JUMBLE®

TIME MACHINE:1984

A Collection of Puzzles from 40 Years Ago!

Henri Arnold

&

Bob Lee

TRIUMPH
BOOKS

For further information, con tact:
Triumph Books LLC
814 North Franklin Street
Chicago, Illinois 60610
Phone: (312) 337-0747
www.triumphbooks.com

Printed in U.S.A.

ISBN: 978-1-63727-389-0

Design by Sue Knopf

CONTENTS

JUMBLE®

TIME MACHINE: 1984

CLASSIC
PUZZLES

JUMBLE®

Unscramble these four Jumbles, one letter
to each square, to form four ordinary words.

LAVIT

CUMSI

TIENNY

CLIFEK

WHY HE INSISTED
ON WEARING
SEAT BELTS.

Now arrange the circled letters
to form the surprise answer, as
suggested by the above cartoon.

Print answer here TO ◯◯◯◯◯ HIS ◯◯◯

JUMBLE®

Unscramble these four Jumbles, one letter
to each square, to form four ordinary words.

RUPOC

VARAL

RAWHOR

BOLGEN

HOW MANY POUNDS OF
LIMBURGER CHEESE
DO YOU WANT?

Now arrange the circled letters
to form the surprise answer, as
suggested by the above cartoon.

Print answer here ◯ "◯◯◯◯"

JUMBLE®

Unscramble these four Jumbles, one letter
to each square, to form four ordinary words.

NELOB

HESAF

LEGGIG

NIFTEC

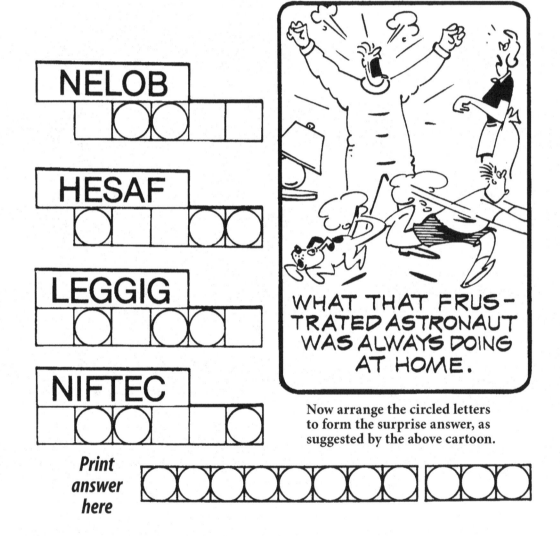

WHAT THAT FRUS-
TRATED ASTRONAUT
WAS ALWAYS DOING
AT HOME.

Now arrange the circled letters
to form the surprise answer, as
suggested by the above cartoon.

*Print
answer
here*

JUMBLE®

Unscramble these four Jumbles, one letter to each square, to form four ordinary words.

STACE

NARBD

GETURT

BUCTAD

It sure took nerve to get where he got

ALTHOUGH MAN DOES NOT LIVE BY BREAD ALONE, HE MAY GET BY ON THIS.

Now arrange the circled letters to form the surprise answer, as suggested by the above cartoon.

Print answer here " ◯◯◯◯◯ "

JUMBLE®

Unscramble these four Jumbles, one letter to each square, to form four ordinary words.

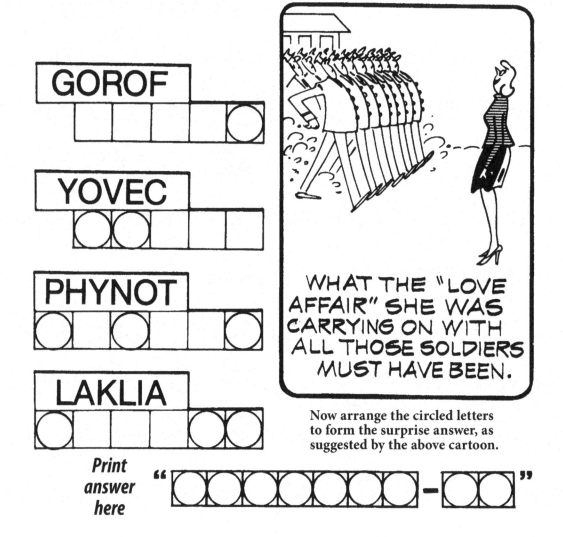

GOROF

YOVEC

PHYNOT

LAKLIA

WHAT THE "LOVE AFFAIR" SHE WAS CARRYING ON WITH ALL THOSE SOLDIERS MUST HAVE BEEN.

Now arrange the circled letters to form the surprise answer, as suggested by the above cartoon.

Print answer here " ◯◯◯◯◯◯◯ – ◯◯ "

JUMBLE®

Unscramble these four Jumbles, one letter
to each square, to form four ordinary words.

ULARR

LABAN

WUNSIE

PORTIM

A FEELING YOU GET
WHEN YOU OPEN YOUR
MAIL ON THE FIRST
OF THE MONTH.

Now arrange the circled letters
to form the surprise answer, as
suggested by the above cartoon.

Print answer here " ◯◯◯◯ - ◯◯◯◯ "

JUMBLE®

Unscramble these four Jumbles, one letter
to each square, to form four ordinary words.

EVVER

LEBLE

GICART

YARWIA

WHAT THEY CALLED
THE MAN WHO PUT
GLASS INTO THE
IGLOO WINDOWS.

Now arrange the circled letters
to form the surprise answer, as
suggested by the above cartoon.

Print answer here   THE "◯◯◯◯◯◯◯"

JUMBLE®

Unscramble these four Jumbles, one letter to each square, to form four ordinary words.

GALEE

SYSAG

TINEKT

STYMIC

WHAT THAT LONG TOUR MADE HIM.

Now arrange the circled letters to form the surprise answer, as suggested by the above cartoon.

Print answer here "◯◯◯" ◯◯◯◯

JUMBLE®

Unscramble these four Jumbles, one letter
to each square, to form four ordinary words.

ORVAS

TWAHR

WOFELL

TEXMEP

WHAT HIS NEIGHBOR
SAID WHEN HE
SHOWED OFF HIS NEW
LAWN EQUIPMENT.

Now arrange the circled letters
to form the surprise answer, as
suggested by the above cartoon.

Print
answer
here "⎵⎵⎵⎵⎵" ⎵⎵⎵⎵⎵ TO
YOU

JUMBLE®

Unscramble these four Jumbles, one letter to each square, to form four ordinary words.

OXTIN

SINUM

HARANG

INGRIF

WHAT THOSE BOXERS ENGAGED IN WHILE HAVING A FEW DRINKS.

Now arrange the circled letters to form the surprise answer, as suggested by the above cartoon.

Print answer here

" ◯◯◯ " ◯◯◯◯◯◯◯◯◯

JUMBLE®

Unscramble these four Jumbles, one letter
to each square, to form four ordinary words.

BODUT

YAMOF

VEEVOL

MUDINS

JEWELRY

WHEN SHE ASKED
FOR A DIAMOND,
HE TURNED THIS.

Now arrange the circled letters
to form the surprise answer, as
suggested by the above cartoon.

Print answer here " ⃝⃝⃝⃝⃝ " ⃝⃝⃝⃝

JUMBLE®

Unscramble these four Jumbles, one letter to each square, to form four ordinary words.

LORBI

HARAJ

KELLIY

SPATOL

ORTHOPEDIC SURGEONS MUST BE LUCKY WHEN THEY GET THIS.

Now arrange the circled letters to form the surprise answer, as suggested by the above cartoon.

Print answer here

○○○ THE " ○○○○○○ "

JUMBLE®

Unscramble these four Jumbles, one letter
to each square, to form four ordinary words.

BREEL

TRIDY

FISHMA

KLAYEC

HOW SHE LOVED
THE CARDIOLOGIST.

Now arrange the circled letters
to form the surprise answer, as
suggested by the above cartoon.

*Print answer
here* WITH ☐◯◯◯☐ HER ◯◯◯◯◯◯

JUMBLE®

Unscramble these four Jumbles, one letter
to each square, to form four ordinary words.

KEREC

AXMMI

SAYMUL

EXLANF

Stop!

WHAT THE ROBBER
SAID AS HE MADE
HIS GETAWAY.

Now arrange the circled letters
to form the surprise answer, as
suggested by the above cartoon.

Print answer here " ◯◯◯◯◯ " BY A ◯◯◯◯

JUMBLE®

Unscramble these four Jumbles, one letter
to each square, to form four ordinary words.

SOINY
◯◯◯ ◯◯

MENGO
☐☐◯◯◯

YABSUW
◯☐◯☐◯☐

TEKLET
◯☐◯☐☐◯

EVEN MORE FUN
THAN HAVING A
VACATION IS
HAVING THIS.

Now arrange the circled letters
to form the surprise answer, as
suggested by the above cartoon.

*Print
answer
here* THE ◯◯◯◯◯ ◯◯◯◯ ◯◯◯

JUMBLE®

Unscramble these four Jumbles, one letter to each square, to form four ordinary words.

THACC

FETHY

ZELZIF

GLARBE

WHAT THE GUY WHO THOUGHT HE WAS A WIT WAS.

Now arrange the circled letters to form the surprise answer, as suggested by the above cartoon.

Print answer here

ONLY

17

JUMBLE®

Unscramble these four Jumbles, one letter
to each square, to form four ordinary words.

SEHCS

NUWDE

YERSIM

WUNTAL

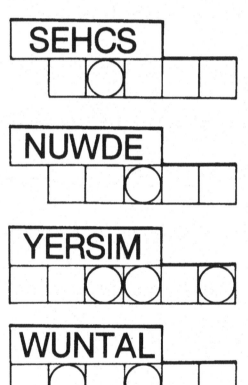

SHE ADMITTED
SHE WAS FORTY
BUT SHE DIDN'T
DO THIS.

Now arrange the circled letters
to form the surprise answer, as
suggested by the above cartoon.

Print answer here

JUMBLE®

Unscramble these four Jumbles, one letter
to each square, to form four ordinary words.

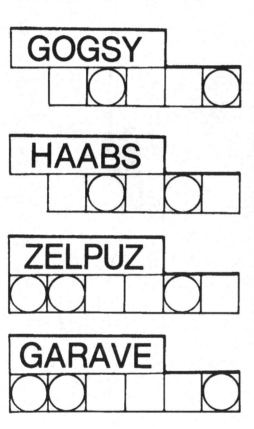

GOGSY

HAABS

ZELPUZ

GARAVE

WHAT HE SAID
THAT SO-CALLED
BARLEY SOUP WAS.

Now arrange the circled letters
to form the surprise answer, as
suggested by the above cartoon.

**Print answer
here**

19

JUMBLE ®

Unscramble these four Jumbles, one letter
to each square, to form four ordinary words.

WHOSY

MOWNE

ATJECK

SALWAY

WHAT THE TALKING
CAT SAID EVERY
TIME ITS MASTER
RETURNED HOME.

Now arrange the circled letters
to form the surprise answer, as
suggested by the above cartoon.

*Print answer
here* ○○○○ ' ○ " ○○○ " ?

JUMBLE®

Unscramble these four Jumbles, one letter to each square, to form four ordinary words.

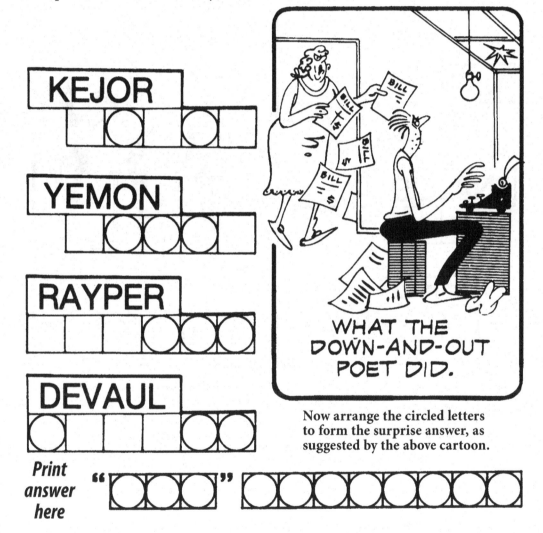

KEJOR

YEMON

RAYPER

DEVAUL

WHAT THE DOWN-AND-OUT POET DID.

Now arrange the circled letters to form the surprise answer, as suggested by the above cartoon.

Print answer here " ⃝⃝⃝ " ⃝⃝⃝⃝⃝⃝⃝⃝⃝

JUMBLE®

Unscramble these four Jumbles, one letter
to each square, to form four ordinary words.

MAWPS

NAJOB

NERRED

EGMAIP

AT WHAT AGE
WERE THEY
MARRIED?

Now arrange the circled letters
to form the surprise answer, as
suggested by the above cartoon.

*Print
answer
here*   AT THE "⬡⬡⬡⬡⬡⬡⬡–⬡⬡⬡"

JUMBLE®

Unscramble these four Jumbles, one letter
to each square, to form four ordinary words.

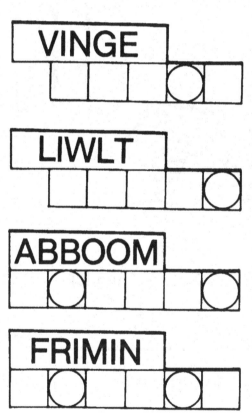

VINGE

LIWLT

ABBOOM

FRIMIN

How about joining us?

No . . . not for me

WHAT THE SOLITARY
PAWNBROKER
UNDOUBTEDLY WAS.

Now arrange the circled letters
to form the surprise answer, as
suggested by the above cartoon.

Print answer here   A " ◯◯◯◯◯◯ "

JUMBLE®

Unscramble these four Jumbles, one letter to each square, to form four ordinary words.

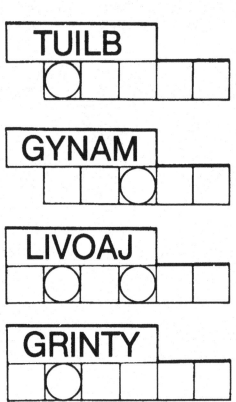

TUILB

GYNAM

LIVOAJ

GRINTY

COULD THIS BE WHY HE WAS A JAILBIRD?

Now arrange the circled letters to form the surprise answer, as suggested by the above cartoon.

Print answer here "  "

JUMBLE®

Unscramble these four Jumbles, one letter
to each square, to form four ordinary words.

ET TIL

GORRI

MELTIG

NIWWON

WHAT HAPPENED
TO THE BELL THAT
FELL INTO THE
WATER?

Now arrange the circled letters
to form the surprise answer, as
suggested by the above cartoon.

Print
answer
here

IT WAS "◯◯◯◯◯◯◯◯" ◯◯◯

JUMBLE®

Unscramble these four Jumbles, one letter
to each square, to form four ordinary words.

LASIE

VAINE

DUBUSE

TUPIRD

I love game

WHY IS VENISON
SO EXPENSIVE?

Now arrange the circled letters
to form the surprise answer, as
suggested by the above cartoon.

Print answer here ◯◯'◯ "◯◯◯◯◯"

JUMBLE®

TIME MACHINE: 1984

DAILY
PUZZLES

JUMBLE®

Unscramble these four Jumbles, one letter
to each square, to form four ordinary words.

KLANB

ARCTT

ADUMAR

MUGLEE

WHAT HAPPENED TO THE
PLASTIC SURGEON WHO
WAS WORKING IN AN
OVERHEATED
OPERATING ROOM?

Now arrange the circled letters
to form the surprise answer, as
suggested by the above cartoon.

Print answer here   HE ⬭⬭⬭⬭⬭⬭

JUMBLE®

Unscramble these four Jumbles, one letter to each square, to form four ordinary words.

ORDOB

HIEWL

YORPOL

DIRAUM

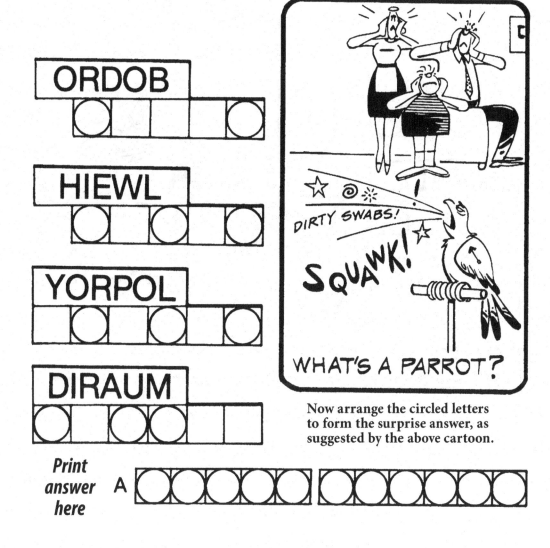

DIRTY SWABS!

SQUAWK!

WHAT'S A PARROT?

Now arrange the circled letters to form the surprise answer, as suggested by the above cartoon.

Print answer here   A

JUMBLE®

Unscramble these four Jumbles, one letter
to each square, to form four ordinary words.

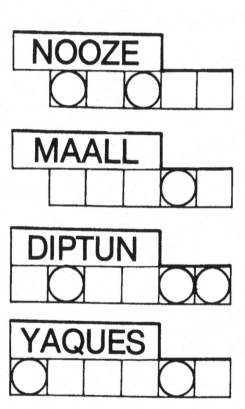

NOOZE

MAALL

DIPTUN

YAQUES

LOVES SKIN
DIVING.

Now arrange the circled letters
to form the surprise answer, as
suggested by the above cartoon.

Print answer here   A

JUMBLE®

Unscramble these four Jumbles, one letter
to each square, to form four ordinary words.

SHOWE

HECKE

DRIZAL

LIZZES

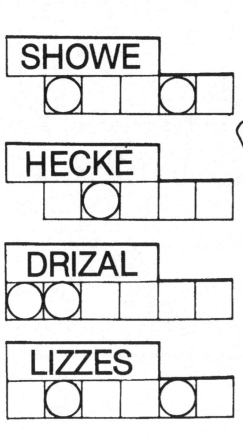

WHAT HIS RICH
UNCLE WHO WAS A
FAMOUS ARTIST KNEW
HOW TO DRAW BEST.

Now arrange the circled letters
to form the surprise answer, as
suggested by the above cartoon.

Print answer here

JUMBLE®

Unscramble these four Jumbles, one letter to each square, to form four ordinary words.

DELAL

KUSYD

COLLEA

SUMPAC

He's sure gone far

HOW THE WEIGHING MACHINE TYCOON STARTED IN BUSINESS.

Now arrange the circled letters to form the surprise answer, as suggested by the above cartoon.

Print answer here   ON A ☐☐☐☐☐☐ ☐☐☐☐☐

JUMBLE®

Unscramble these four Jumbles, one letter to each square, to form four ordinary words.

RYKUM

BOSEE

LURCUN

STIPTY

HOW TO GET YOUR WIFE TO BAKE THOSE DELICIOUS ROLLS.

Now arrange the circled letters to form the surprise answer, as suggested by the above cartoon.

Print answer here ◯◯◯◯◯◯ HER ◯◯

JUMBLE®

Unscramble these four Jumbles, one letter to each square, to form four ordinary words.

NIRED

YUCIJ

REEPAM

NIFTIE

WHAT THE FRIGHTENED ROCK WAS.

Now arrange the circled letters to form the surprise answer, as suggested by the above cartoon.

Print answer here " ◯◯◯◯◯◯◯◯◯ "

JUMBLE®

Unscramble these four Jumbles, one letter
to each square, to form four ordinary words.

ACTUD

ESSOU

FRYTAC

TYKONT

WHAT TO DO
WHEN A PLUG
DOESN'T FIT.

Now arrange the circled letters
to form the surprise answer, as
suggested by the above cartoon.

Print answer here "  "

35

JUMBLE®

Unscramble these four Jumbles, one letter
to each square, to form four ordinary words.

ILLAC

IGNAT

TYDWAR

CUNNEA

WHAT THEY WERE
DOING ON THAT
TELEVISED BALLET.

Now arrange the circled letters
to form the surprise answer, as
suggested by the above cartoon.

Print
answer
here

◯◯◯◯◯◯◯ ON ◯◯◯

JUMBLE®

Unscramble these four Jumbles, one letter
to each square, to form four ordinary words.

CINEE

INVEX

BLIRME

INBENG

Sorry, Ronald—you're
not my type

HOW THE VAMPIRE
LOVED.

Now arrange the circled letters
to form the surprise answer, as
suggested by the above cartoon.

Print answer here   " "

JUMBLE®

Unscramble these four Jumbles, one letter
to each square, to form four ordinary words.

FRASC

WELJE

DRAWZI

KEBTUC

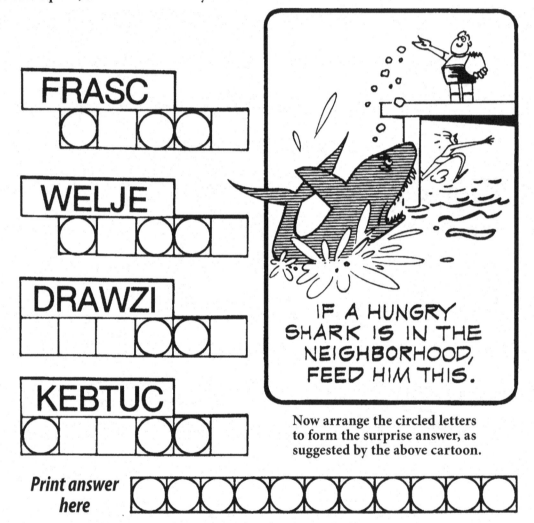

IF A HUNGRY
SHARK IS IN THE
NEIGHBORHOOD,
FEED HIM THIS.

Now arrange the circled letters
to form the surprise answer, as
suggested by the above cartoon.

*Print answer
here*

JUMBLE®

Unscramble these four Jumbles, one letter to each square, to form four ordinary words.

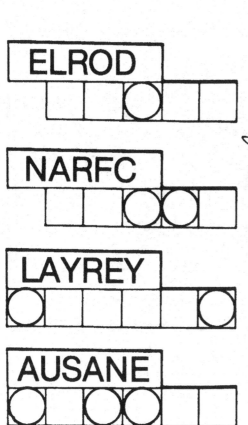

ELROD

NARFC

LAYREY

AUSANE

Can't take too many precautions

WHAT THE UMBRELLA MERCHANT WAS SAVING HIS MONEY FOR.

Now arrange the circled letters to form the surprise answer, as suggested by the above cartoon.

Print answer here   A

JUMBLE®

Unscramble these four Jumbles, one letter to each square, to form four ordinary words.

PUBYM

CRAID

TALBOC

DOINIE

Guess I won't go to work today

Hurray, no school!

HOW DOES JACK FROST GET TO WORK?

Now arrange the circled letters to form the surprise answer, as suggested by the above cartoon.

Print answer here ⟨ ⟩ " ⟨ ⟩ "

JUMBLE®

Unscramble these four Jumbles, one letter
to each square, to form four ordinary words.

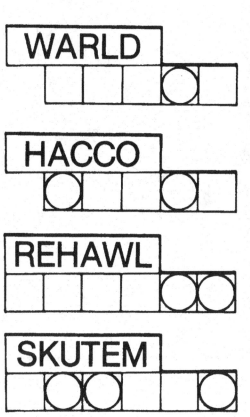

WARLD

HACCO

REHAWL

SKUTEM

THE SHIP DOCKED
NEAR THE BARBERSHOP
BECAUSE THEY ALL
NEEDED THIS.

Now arrange the circled letters
to form the surprise answer, as
suggested by the above cartoon.

Print answer here

JUMBLE.

Unscramble these four Jumbles, one letter
to each square, to form four ordinary words.

THILG

KUSHY

CEEDOD

NICRIO

HONK! HONK!

Who's afraid?!

THE TURKEY CROSSED
THE ROAD TO
PROVE THIS.

Now arrange the circled letters
to form the surprise answer, as
suggested by the above cartoon.

*Print
answer
here*   ◯◯ WASN'T " ◯◯◯◯◯◯◯ "

JUMBLE®

Unscramble these four Jumbles, one letter
to each square, to form four ordinary words.

KEWOA

URYMM

SACCUT

CEPTIK

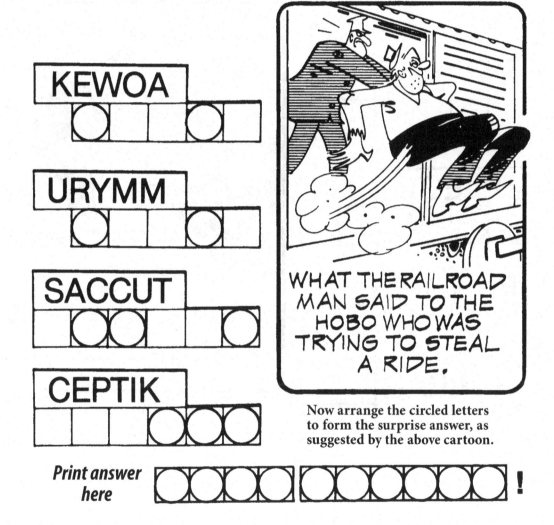

WHAT THE RAILROAD
MAN SAID TO THE
HOBO WHO WAS
TRYING TO STEAL
A RIDE.

Now arrange the circled letters
to form the surprise answer, as
suggested by the above cartoon.

Print answer
here ◯◯◯◯ ◯◯◯◯◯◯ !

JUMBLE®

Unscramble these four Jumbles, one letter
to each square, to form four ordinary words.

DUTOO

FLECT

EDGERD

BORRAH

CRYPTOGRAPHY ROOM

WHAT THE SECRET
AGENT WAS
COMPLAINING OF.

Now arrange the circled letters
to form the surprise answer, as
suggested by the above cartoon.

Print answer here A "◯◯◯◯" IN THE ◯◯◯◯

JUMBLE®

Unscramble these four Jumbles, one letter
to each square, to form four ordinary words.

SOONE

YOWND

BLUBEA

YARNTT

LOONY
BIN

WHY THEY HAD
TO PUT THE
VAMPIRE AWAY.

Now arrange the circled letters
to form the surprise answer, as
suggested by the above cartoon.

Print answer here HE ⬭⬭⬭⬭ ⬭⬭⬭⬭

JUMBLE®

Unscramble these four Jumbles, one letter
to each square, to form four ordinary words.

MOBOL

CEENF

UNSLIM

QUIDIL

WHAT THE DOCTOR
SAID WHEN THE
PATIENT COMPLAINED
OF RINGING IN
HIS EARS.

Now arrange the circled letters
to form the surprise answer, as
suggested by the above cartoon.

Print
answer   YOU'RE ⬡⬡⬡⬡⬡ AS A ⬡⬡⬡⬡
here

JUMBLE®

Unscramble these four Jumbles, one letter to each square, to form four ordinary words.

DITIO

SUDOE

JEDGAG

BRUMEN

Couldn't get a promotion there

HELP WANTED

FUNERAL PARLOR

WHY HE QUIT WORKING AT THE UNDERTAKER'S.

Now arrange the circled letters to form the surprise answer, as suggested by the above cartoon.

Print answer here   IT WAS A ◯◯◯◯-◯◯◯ ◯◯◯

JUMBLE®

Unscramble these four Jumbles, one letter to each square, to form four ordinary words.

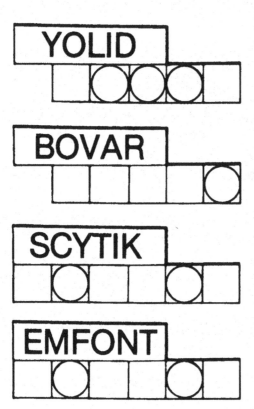

YOLID

BOVAR

SCYTIK

EMFONT

WHEN A VANDAL MADE A HOLE IN THE FENCE AT THE NUDIST CAMP, THE COPS SAID THEY'D DO THIS.

Now arrange the circled letters to form the surprise answer, as suggested by the above cartoon.

Print answer here  IT

JUMBLE®

Unscramble these four Jumbles, one letter
to each square, to form four ordinary words.

PRAID

LAWRC

EXCOBI

NYLARX

WHAT HE GOT WHEN
HE READ THE STORY
ABOUT THOSE
BODY SNATCHERS.

Now arrange the circled letters
to form the surprise answer, as
suggested by the above cartoon.

Print
answer
here

JUMBLE®

Unscramble these four Jumbles, one letter
to each square, to form four ordinary words.

THOOP

BASUQ

NAEVLE

MUGNIP

WHAT "HMS
PINAFORE" COULD
UNDOUBTEDLY BE.

Now arrange the circled letters
to form the surprise answer, as
suggested by the above cartoon.

Print answer
here " ◯◯◯◯ FOR ◯◯◯◯ "

JUMBLE®

Unscramble these four Jumbles, one letter to each square, to form four ordinary words.

NELEK

BROEP

TERVOX

CAYGLE

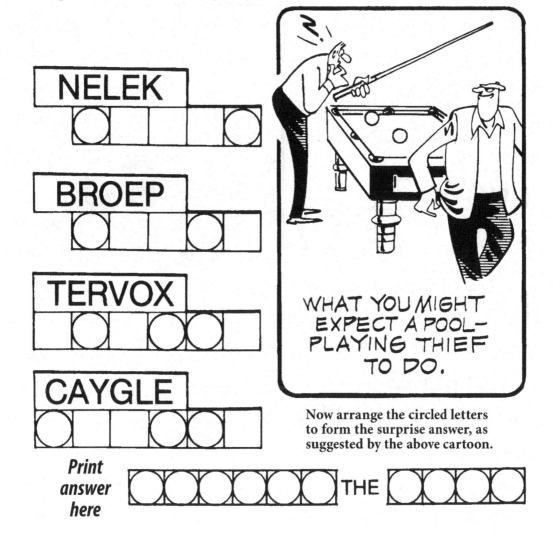

WHAT YOU MIGHT
EXPECT A POOL-
PLAYING THIEF
TO DO.

Now arrange the circled letters to form the surprise answer, as suggested by the above cartoon.

Print answer here ⬡⬡⬡⬡⬡⬡ THE ⬡⬡⬡⬡

JUMBLE®

Unscramble these four Jumbles, one letter
to each square, to form four ordinary words.

EAPEY

RAWFE

BETHIL

VARQUE

WHY SHE DIVED
INTO THE SEA.

Now arrange the circled letters
to form the surprise answer, as
suggested by the above cartoon.

*Print
answer
here*   TO GET A ⬡⬡⬡⬡ IN HER ⬡⬡⬡⬡

JUMBLE®

Unscramble these four Jumbles, one letter to each square, to form four ordinary words.

DAJED

KEVOE

BARNEY

CLITIE

ONE CAT TOLD THE OTHER TO BE CAREFUL LEST HE DO THIS.

Now arrange the circled letters to form the surprise answer, as suggested by the above cartoon.

Print answer here

UP IN THAT

JUMBLE®

Unscramble these four Jumbles, one letter to each square, to form four ordinary words.

NAYLK

BITOR

TESACK

PLAACA

WHAT CHIROPRACTORS CAN EXPECT A LOT OF.

Now arrange the circled letters to form the surprise answer, as suggested by the above cartoon.

Print answer here

JUMBLE®

Unscramble these four Jumbles, one letter to each square, to form four ordinary words.

ELVOG

PORDO

TAJUNY

MINGOH

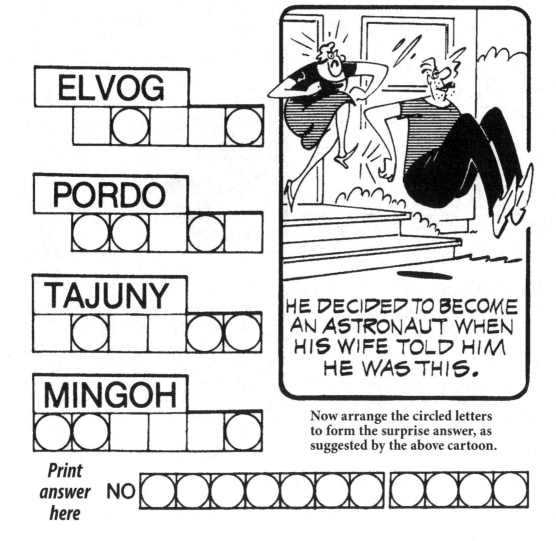

HE DECIDED TO BECOME AN ASTRONAUT WHEN HIS WIFE TOLD HIM HE WAS THIS.

Now arrange the circled letters to form the surprise answer, as suggested by the above cartoon.

Print answer here NO ⬡⬡⬡⬡⬡⬡⬡ ⬡⬡⬡⬡

JUMBLE®

Unscramble these four Jumbles, one letter
to each square, to form four ordinary words.

PINYP

SABIN

TOINNE

DRAFIT

HEALTH CENTER

IF YOU WANT TO
START LOSING WEIGHT,
YOU CAN GET
INITIATED FROM THIS.

Now arrange the circled letters
to form the surprise answer, as
suggested by the above cartoon.

Print answer
here   A "⬡⬡⬡⬡⬡⬡⬡⬡⬡"

JUMBLE®

Unscramble these four Jumbles, one letter
to each square, to form four ordinary words.

CHARP

NACYF

MENIER

RASTUX

WHERE DO
ALL THE
FLEAS GO
IN WINTER?

Now arrange the circled letters
to form the surprise answer, as
suggested by the above cartoon.

Print answer here " ⬡⬡⬡⬡⬡⬡ ⬡⬡ "

JUMBLE®

Unscramble these four Jumbles, one letter to each square, to form four ordinary words.

MIRGE

INAFT

LOMOGY

RUGEDD

THE COFFEE TYCOON DECIDED TO RETIRE BECAUSE HE COULDN'T STAND THIS.

Now arrange the circled letters to form the surprise answer, as suggested by the above cartoon.

Print answer here

THE ⬡⬡⬡⬡⬡ "⬡⬡⬡⬡⬡"

JUMBLE®

Unscramble these four Jumbles, one letter
to each square, to form four ordinary words.

KNACS

LAROF

LUGGEJ

CEPPIT

WHAT HE WHO
LAUGHS LAST OFTEN
DOESN'T DO.

Now arrange the circled letters
to form the surprise answer, as
suggested by the above cartoon.

Print answer here ⬡⬡⬡ THE ⬡⬡⬡⬡

JUMBLE®

Unscramble these four Jumbles, one letter
to each square, to form four ordinary words.

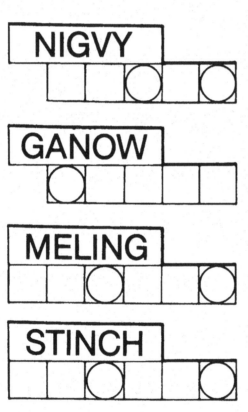

NIGVY

GANOW

MELING

STINCH

EXIT

?

WHAT THE NEAR-
SIGHTED BOXER HAD
TROUBLE FINDING.

Now arrange the circled letters
to form the surprise answer, as
suggested by the above cartoon.

Print answer here THE " ⬡⬡⬡⬡⬡⬡ – ⬡⬡ "

JUMBLE®

Unscramble these four Jumbles, one letter
to each square, to form four ordinary words.

UNHAM

PEROW

LOUBED

SEELAW

WHAT EVE SAID
WHEN ADAM ASKED
WHETHER SHE
STILL LOVED HIM.

Now arrange the circled letters
to form the surprise answer, as
suggested by the above cartoon.

Print answer here ◯◯◯ ◯◯◯◯**?**

JUMBLE®

Unscramble these four Jumbles, one letter
to each square, to form four ordinary words.

THIGE

STYRT

YEUFLE

REGOUM

WHEN IS THE
CHEAPEST TIME TO
PHONE YOUR FRIENDS
BY LONG DISTANCE?

Now arrange the circled letters
to form the surprise answer, as
suggested by the above cartoon.

Print
answer
here

WHEN ⬡⬡⬡⬡'⬡⬡ ⬡⬡⬡

JUMBLE®

Unscramble these four Jumbles, one letter to each square, to form four ordinary words.

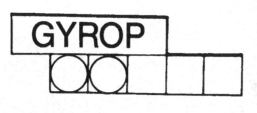

GYROP

RARIF

ROHORR

SEATTE

DID YOU HEAR MY LAST JOKE?

Now arrange the circled letters to form the surprise answer, as suggested by the above cartoon.

Print answer here " ☐☐ ☐☐☐☐ ☐☐ "

JUMBLE®

Unscramble these four Jumbles, one letter to each square, to form four ordinary words.

LAMEY

REBAG

CHERAG

NIPURT

WHAT SOME BEARS
SEEM TO DO IN
WINTERTIME.

Now arrange the circled letters to form the surprise answer, as suggested by the above cartoon.

Print answer here "☐☐-☐☐☐☐☐-☐☐☐☐"

JUMBLE®

Unscramble these four Jumbles, one letter
to each square, to form four ordinary words.

TUMOH

KYACT

GROAND

SMEFLY

THE MAN WHO
STOLE A PUDDING
WAS TAKEN
INTO THIS.

Now arrange the circled letters
to form the surprise answer, as
suggested by the above cartoon.

Print answer here "◯◯◯◯◯◯◯◯"

JUMBLE®

Unscramble these four Jumbles, one letter to each square, to form four ordinary words.

AUPSE

MERFA

NEXETT

TROBEH

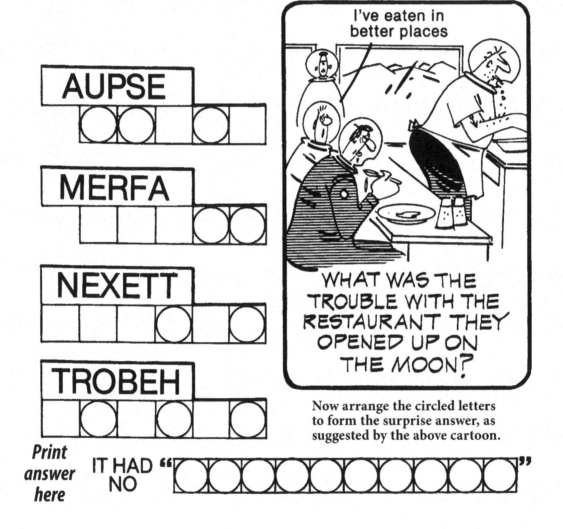

I've eaten in better places

WHAT WAS THE TROUBLE WITH THE RESTAURANT THEY OPENED UP ON THE MOON?

Now arrange the circled letters to form the surprise answer, as suggested by the above cartoon.

Print answer here

IT HAD " ◯◯◯◯◯◯◯◯◯◯ "

JUMBLE®

Unscramble these four Jumbles, one letter
to each square, to form four ordinary words.

ADURF

WANTY

RUHLOY

VAHLIS

WHAT HE SAID WHEN
TEACHER GAVE HIM
AN "F" ON THE
VOCABULARY TEST.

Now arrange the circled letters
to form the surprise answer, as
suggested by the above cartoon.

**Print answer
here** ◯◯◯◯◯◯ ◯◯◯◯ ME

JUMBLE®

Unscramble these four Jumbles, one letter
to each square, to form four ordinary words.

TURSY

JECET

LAYMIN

SEPPOO

WHERE YOU
MIGHT FIND THE
SCHOOLMASTER.

Now arrange the circled letters
to form the surprise answer, as
suggested by the above cartoon.

*Print
answer
here*   IN "THE "

JUMBLE®

Unscramble these four Jumbles, one letter
to each square, to form four ordinary words.

RORYS

HERBT

SULTYS

RUGBBY

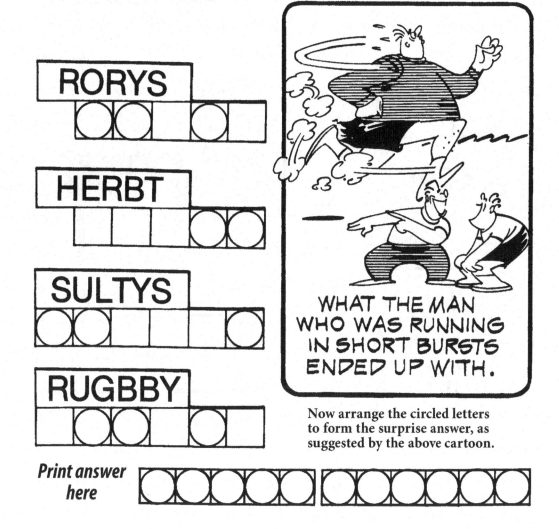

WHAT THE MAN
WHO WAS RUNNING
IN SHORT BURSTS
ENDED UP WITH.

Now arrange the circled letters
to form the surprise answer, as
suggested by the above cartoon.

**Print answer
here**

JUMBLE®

Unscramble these four Jumbles, one letter
to each square, to form four ordinary words.

VANER

WENYL

ELCHEK

TOMMAR

I'm shocked!

WHAT FOUR-LETTER
WORD DO SOME
PEOPLE FIND MOST
OBJECTIONABLE?

Now arrange the circled letters
to form the surprise answer, as
suggested by the above cartoon.

Print answer here " ◯◯◯◯ "

JUMBLE®

Unscramble these four Jumbles, one letter
to each square, to form four ordinary words.

IRATT

CURCO

TABBIR

ENWAKE

Another
best-
seller

WHAT THE
SUCCESSFUL
NOVELIST MUST
HAVE BEEN.

Now arrange the circled letters
to form the surprise answer, as
suggested by the above cartoon.

*Print
answer
here* ON THE "⬡⬡⬡⬡⬡⬡" ⬡⬡⬡⬡⬡

JUMBLE®

Unscramble these four Jumbles, one letter to each square, to form four ordinary words.

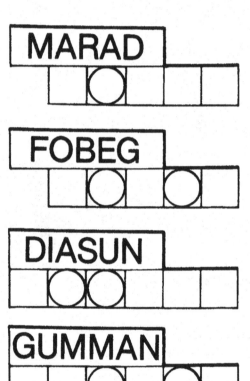

MARAD

FOBEG

DIASUN

GUMMAN

FROM THE SURGEON CAME THESE WORDS.

Now arrange the circled letters to form the surprise answer, as suggested by the above cartoon.

Print answer here " ⬡⬡ , ⬡⬡⬡⬡⬡ ! "

JUMBLE®

Unscramble these four Jumbles, one letter
to each square, to form four ordinary words.

ROHTT

ILFOO

GIANAU

UMLUTT

Won't he ever forget it?!

THE IMPRESSION MADE
ON ONE WHO'S BEEN
IN THE NAVY MIGHT
BE QUITE LASTING.

Now arrange the circled letters
to form the surprise answer, as
suggested by the above cartoon.

Print answer here

JUMBLE®

Unscramble these four Jumbles, one letter
to each square, to form four ordinary words.

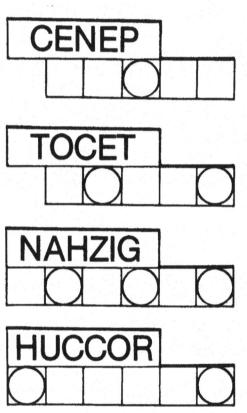

CENEP

TOCET

NAHZIG

HUCCOR

FISHING MAY BE
A "DISEASE," BUT
IT'S NOT NECES-
SARILY THIS.

Now arrange the circled letters
to form the surprise answer, as
suggested by the above cartoon.

Print answer here "⟨ ⟩"

JUMBLE®

Unscramble these four Jumbles, one letter
to each square, to form four ordinary words.

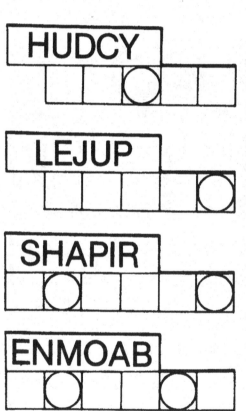

HUDCY

LEJUP

SHAPIR

ENMOAB

DID THEY CALL
HER THIS BECAUSE
SHE HAD A
HEART OF STONE?

Now arrange the circled letters
to form the surprise answer, as
suggested by the above cartoon.

Print answer here

JUMBLE®

Unscramble these four Jumbles, one letter to each square, to form four ordinary words.

UGOBS

KNOTE

LIRMAN

MOANEY

WHAT MUCH SO—CALLED PRESIDENTIAL TIMBER OFTEN IS.

Now arrange the circled letters to form the surprise answer, as suggested by the above cartoon.

Print answer here

"   "

JUMBLE®

Unscramble these four Jumbles, one letter to each square, to form four ordinary words.

LELIS

PAUNC

SUCLEM

SLAQUL

One after another. . .

HOW THAT DON JUAN TREATED ALL WOMEN.

Now arrange the circled letters to form the surprise answer, as suggested by the above cartoon.

Print answer here

" "

JUMBLE®

Unscramble these four Jumbles, one letter
to each square, to form four ordinary words.

INSIF

YOHEN

KOHOED

UNTEAB

He's got muscles between
his ears, too

WHERE THE CONCEITED
WEIGHT LIFTER
LET HIS BODY GO.

Now arrange the circled letters
to form the surprise answer, as
suggested by the above cartoon.

Print answer here

JUMBLE®

Unscramble these four Jumbles, one letter to each square, to form four ordinary words.

GOARC

HAIKK

LOUTTE

TIMOON

WHAT THAT BAKERY TYCOON WAS.

Now arrange the circled letters to form the surprise answer, as suggested by the above cartoon.

Print answer here   ONE ☐☐☐☐☐☐ ☐☐☐☐☐☐☐

JUMBLE®

Unscramble these four Jumbles, one letter
to each square, to form four ordinary words.

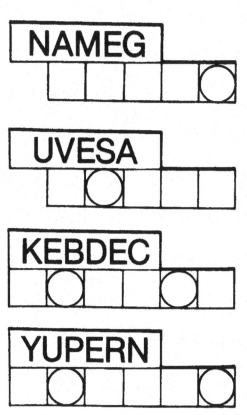

NAMEG

UVESA

KEBDEC

YUPERN

WHAT HER APPEAL
SPRANG FROM.

Now arrange the circled letters
to form the surprise answer, as
suggested by the above cartoon.

Print answer here   HER " ☐☐☐ ☐☐☐ "

JUMBLE®

Unscramble these four Jumbles, one letter
to each square, to form four ordinary words.

RYDYL

DONSY

NAILET

BELNAG

WHAT HER IDEAL
BECAME AFTER SHE
MARRIED HIM.

Now arrange the circled letters
to form the surprise answer, as
suggested by the above cartoon.

Print answer here AN ⬡⬡⬡⬡⬡⬡

JUMBLE®

Unscramble these four Jumbles, one letter to each square, to form four ordinary words.

ELLAP

RAPOE

INSOUC

CAPTEK

Oh, not again!

WHAT THAT OLD-TIME GARAGE MECHANIC WAS BOTHERED WITH.

Now arrange the circled letters to form the surprise answer, as suggested by the above cartoon.

Print answer here

" ◯◯◯◯◯ " ◯◯◯◯◯

JUMBLE®

Unscramble these four Jumbles, one letter to each square, to form four ordinary words.

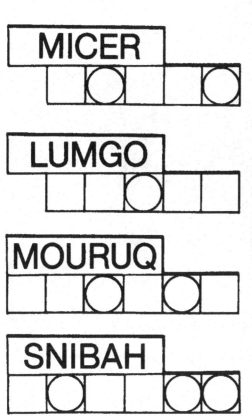

MICER

LUMGO

MOURUQ

SNIBAH

IN WHICH IT'S DIFFICULT TO ROW— WHEN YOU "MANIPULATE" HUGE OARS.

Now arrange the circled letters to form the surprise answer, as suggested by the above cartoon.

Print answer here   A " ⬚⬚⬚⬚⬚ ⬚⬚⬚ "

JUMBLE®

Unscramble these four Jumbles, one letter
to each square, to form four ordinary words.

ECSEA

PLONY

JOACLE

NATTIC

WHAT THE ALERT
WAITER ALWAYS WAS.

Now arrange the circled letters
to form the surprise answer, as
suggested by the above cartoon.

**Print answer
here**   ON HIS " ☐☐☐ " ☐☐☐☐

JUMBLE®

Unscramble these four Jumbles, one letter
to each square, to form four ordinary words.

VARGE

DIEFT

DIBOLE

CAMIAN

HE THOUGHT HIS NEW
COMPUTER
WAS GOING TO GIVE
HIM THIS KIND
OF AN ILLNESS.

Now arrange the circled letters
to form the surprise answer, as
suggested by the above cartoon.

Print
answer   A " ◯◯◯◯◯◯◯◯◯ " ONE
here

JUMBLE®

Unscramble these four Jumbles, one letter
to each square, to form four ordinary words.

GALOT

SMUCA

CUDINE

SAHDIR

WHAT THAT CRAZY
ARTIST MADE OF
HIS MODEL.

Now arrange the circled letters
to form the surprise answer, as
suggested by the above cartoon.

Print answer here

JUMBLE®

Unscramble these four Jumbles, one letter to each square, to form four ordinary words.

SUYFS

YATTS

SPEEXO

HAREMM

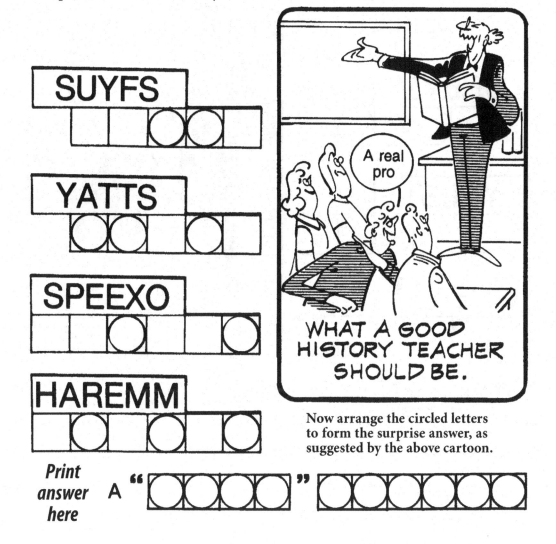

A real pro

WHAT A GOOD HISTORY TEACHER SHOULD BE.

Now arrange the circled letters to form the surprise answer, as suggested by the above cartoon.

Print answer here A " ⬭⬭⬭⬭ " ⬭⬭⬭⬭⬭⬭⬭

JUMBLE ®

Unscramble these four Jumbles, one letter
to each square, to form four ordinary words.

CREYM

YULST

GREATT

PANNKI

Here's a
penny for
you, my
good man

WHAT A CENT TIP
WOULD CERTAINLY
MAKE THESE DAYS.

Now arrange the circled letters
to form the surprise answer, as
suggested by the above cartoon.

Print answer here   A " ⟨◯◯◯◯◯◯◯◯◯⟩ "

JUMBLE®

Unscramble these four Jumbles, one letter
to each square, to form four ordinary words.

CUDEN

SEGUS

MOVULE

ANQUIT

I'm
hungry

How
much
longer?

A WORD OF FIVE
LETTERS THE LAST
FOUR OF WHICH
ARE UNNECESSARY.

Now arrange the circled letters
to form the surprise answer, as
suggested by the above cartoon.

Print answer here " ☐ - ☐☐☐☐ "

JUMBLE®

Unscramble these four Jumbles, one letter
to each square, to form four ordinary words.

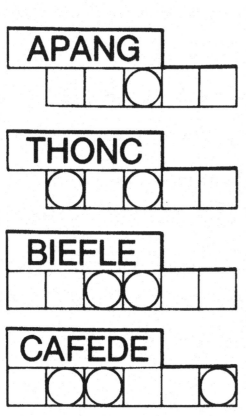

APANG

THONC

BIEFLE

CAFEDE

A girl in every port

THE SAILOR'S MANY
ROMANCES WERE
JUST THIS.

Now arrange the circled letters
to form the surprise answer, as
suggested by the above cartoon.

Print answer here "◯◯◯◯◯ – ◯◯◯"

JUMBLE®

Unscramble these four Jumbles, one letter
to each square, to form four ordinary words.

GELBI

DEPIT

THENUR

DEFLAB

Should I or
shouldn't I?

WHAT TO DO
WHEN YOU GET THE
FEELING THAT YOU
WANT TO SPLURGE.

Now arrange the circled letters
to form the surprise answer, as
suggested by the above cartoon.

Print
answer
here   ⬡⬡⬡ IT IN THE " ⬡⬡⬡ - ⬡⬡⬡ "

JUMBLE®

Unscramble these four Jumbles, one letter to each square, to form four ordinary words.

EUJIC

JAROM

PENXED

TISMEY

There's a slight discrepancy in your account!

IRS

WHAT THE GOVERN-MENT EXPECTS TO GET FROM INCOME TAXES.

Now arrange the circled letters to form the surprise answer, as suggested by the above cartoon.

Print answer here

" ◯◯◯◯◯ ◯◯◯◯◯◯◯ "

JUMBLE®

Unscramble these four Jumbles, one letter to each square, to form four ordinary words.

KALEF

GUAVE

ZOAMAN

GEEREM

LIGHTLY GIVES YOU THE GO-AHEAD.

Now arrange the circled letters to form the surprise answer, as suggested by the above cartoon.

Print answer here

JUMBLE®

Unscramble these four Jumbles, one letter
to each square, to form four ordinary words.

NITLE

INWET

ENFRYZ

ALCIME

He's certainly becoming
well-known

BOOKS

WHAT THE AUTHOR'S
PSEUDONYM WAS.

Now arrange the circled letters
to form the surprise answer, as
suggested by the above cartoon.

Print
answer
here

HIS " ⃝⃝⃝⃝⃝ " ⃝⃝⃝⃝

JUMBLE®

Unscramble these four Jumbles, one letter
to each square, to form four ordinary words.

ORFEC

HIDUM

WARTOD

WHEPEN

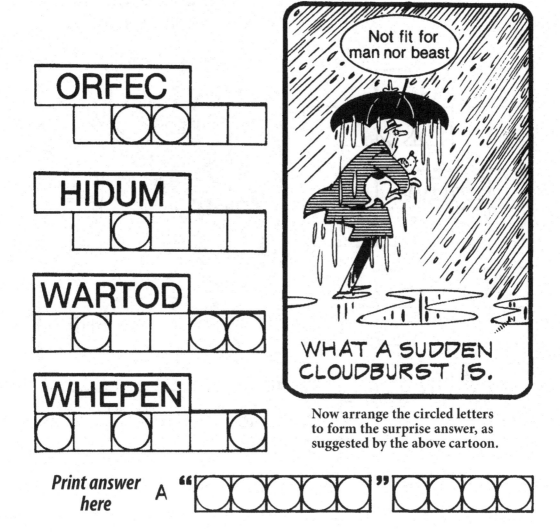

Not fit for
man nor beast

WHAT A SUDDEN
CLOUDBURST IS.

Now arrange the circled letters
to form the surprise answer, as
suggested by the above cartoon.

Print answer
here   A " ◯◯◯◯◯ " ◯◯◯◯

JUMBLE®

Unscramble these four Jumbles, one letter
to each square, to form four ordinary words.

ORFUL

LEHEW

TIPEOA

CLAMBE

Can't do a thing with it

WHAT SHE DID
EVERY TIME SHE
WASHED HER
HAIR.

Now arrange the circled letters
to form the surprise answer, as
suggested by the above cartoon.

Print answer here ⬡⬡⬡⬡⬡ HER ⬡⬡⬡

JUMBLE®

Unscramble these four Jumbles, one letter to each square, to form four ordinary words.

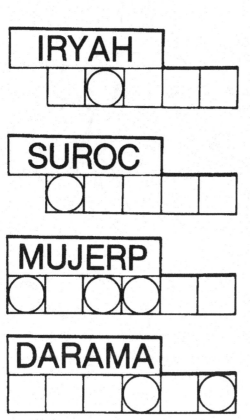

IRYAH

SUROC

MUJERP

DARAMA

There he goes again

WHAT A SLEEP-WALKER'S HABIT USUALLY IS.

Now arrange the circled letters to form the surprise answer, as suggested by the above cartoon.

Print answer here

JUMBLE®

Unscramble these four Jumbles, one letter to each square, to form four ordinary words.

CLUHG

SEROU

PATELA

BEGBIT

WHAT BATHING GIRLS MIGHT BE.

Now arrange the circled letters to form the surprise answer, as suggested by the above cartoon.

Print answer here " IN ⬡⬡⬡⬡⬡⬡ ⬡⬡⬡⬡ "

JUMBLE®

Unscramble these four Jumbles, one letter to each square, to form four ordinary words.

YINKK

ZAWLT

LURIAB

ACDAFE

WHAT A QUACK DOCTOR USUALLY TRIES TO DO.

Now arrange the circled letters to form the surprise answer, as suggested by the above cartoon.

Print answer here ◯◯◯◯ **THE** ◯◯◯

JUMBLE®

Unscramble these four Jumbles, one letter
to each square, to form four ordinary words.

STEAE

TENFO

COSMAT

NEPELS

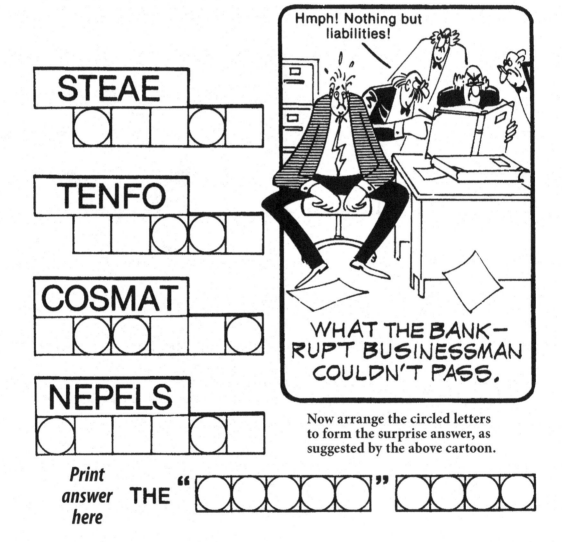

Hmph! Nothing but
liabilities!

WHAT THE BANK-
RUPT BUSINESSMAN
COULDN'T PASS.

Now arrange the circled letters
to form the surprise answer, as
suggested by the above cartoon.

Print
answer
here   THE "◯◯◯◯◯" ◯◯◯◯

JUMBLE®

Unscramble these four Jumbles, one letter
to each square, to form four ordinary words.

TUDAL

GIERT

FLOUBE

REVONG

WHAT SOME
SECRETARIES
HAVE TO TAKE.

Now arrange the circled letters
to form the surprise answer, as
suggested by the above cartoon.

Print
answer
here

A ◯◯◯ FOR " ◯◯◯◯◯◯◯ "

JUMBLE®

Unscramble these four Jumbles, one letter
to each square, to form four ordinary words.

ETIRP

BOYHB

CUSTOC

ORMMEY

HOW YOU HAVE TO
LEARN TO TAKE
CARE OF A BABY.

Now arrange the circled letters
to form the surprise answer, as
suggested by the above cartoon.

Print answer
here

FROM THE ◯◯◯◯◯◯ ◯◯

JUMBLE®

Unscramble these four Jumbles, one letter to each square, to form four ordinary words.

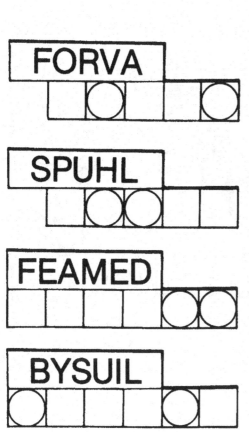

FORVA

SPUHL

FEAMED

BYSUIL

HELD UP IN BAD WEATHER.

Now arrange the circled letters to form the surprise answer, as suggested by the above cartoon.

Print answer here AN ⟨☐☐☐☐☐☐☐☐⟩

JUMBLE®

Unscramble these four Jumbles, one letter to each square, to form four ordinary words.

SHURC

KNEWA

BOPISH

FITONY

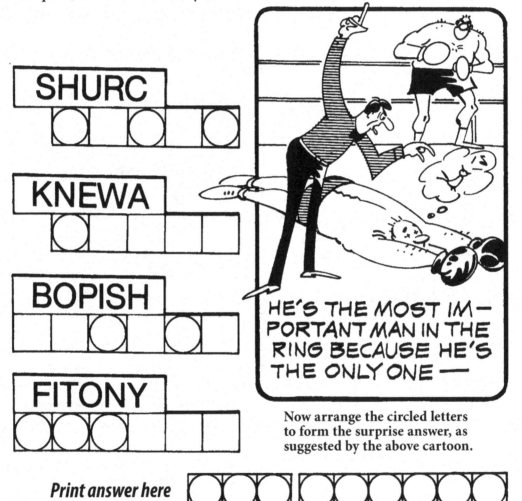

HE'S THE MOST IM— PORTANT MAN IN THE RING BECAUSE HE'S THE ONLY ONE—

Now arrange the circled letters to form the surprise answer, as suggested by the above cartoon.

Print answer here

JUMBLE®

Unscramble these four Jumbles, one letter to each square, to form four ordinary words.

TANGE

HANEY

FRUIPY

REBURB

Gorgeous!

WHAT A FASHION MODEL MIGHT FIGURE ON.

Now arrange the circled letters to form the surprise answer, as suggested by the above cartoon.

Print answer here

JUMBLE®

Unscramble these four Jumbles, one letter
to each square, to form four ordinary words.

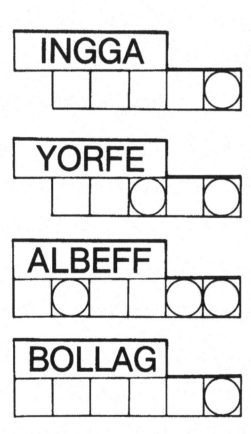

INGGA

YORFE

ALBEFF

BOLLAG

DOES IT ALL COME
FROM AN ALLERGY?

Now arrange the circled letters
to form the surprise answer, as
suggested by the above cartoon.

Print answer here "  "

JUMBLE®

Unscramble these four Jumbles, one letter
to each square, to form four ordinary words.

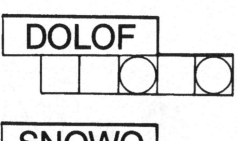

DOLOF

SNOWO

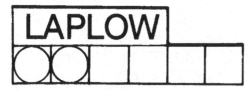

LAPLOW

SHINIF

WHAT THAT
PEEPING TOM WAS.

Now arrange the circled letters
to form the surprise answer, as
suggested by the above cartoon.

Print answer here A

JUMBLE®

Unscramble these four Jumbles, one letter
to each square, to form four ordinary words.

PYLAP

HARCI

TRIVED

NUHRGY

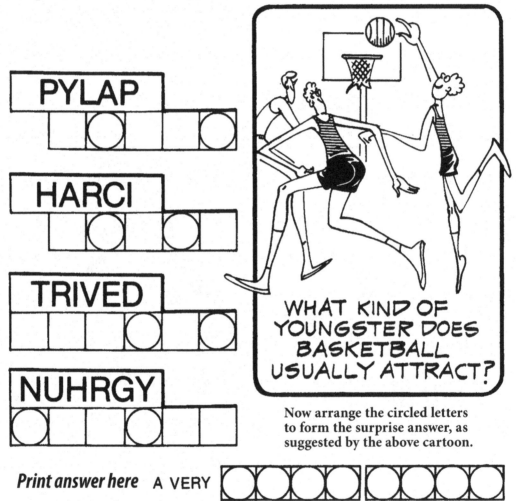

WHAT KIND OF
YOUNGSTER DOES
BASKETBALL
USUALLY ATTRACT?

Now arrange the circled letters
to form the surprise answer, as
suggested by the above cartoon.

Print answer here   A VERY ◯◯◯◯ ◯◯◯◯

JUMBLE®

Unscramble these four Jumbles, one letter
to each square, to form four ordinary words.

RYFIA

TELIE

REDOWP

CLAUHN

Here—have some pills

WHAT THEY CALLED
THAT CROOKED
POLITICIAN
TURNED DOCTOR.

Now arrange the circled letters
to form the surprise answer, as
suggested by the above cartoon.

Print
answer
here

THE ⬡⬡⬡⬡ "⬡⬡⬡⬡⬡⬡"

JUMBLE®

Unscramble these four Jumbles, one letter to each square, to form four ordinary words.

TIDOT

WETHA

RYCKIT

WHALLO

HOW CHILDREN ARRIVE AT YOUR DOOR TONIGHT.

Now arrange the circled letters to form the surprise answer, as suggested by the above cartoon.

Print answer here EVERY " ☐☐☐☐☐ " ☐☐☐

JUMBLE®

Unscramble these four Jumbles, one letter to each square, to form four ordinary words.

SCAIB

ACCOO

HIPLAC

ZEERIF

Now arrange the circled letters to form the surprise answer, as suggested by the above cartoon.

Print answer here " ⃝⃝⃝⃝ "

JUMBLE®

Unscramble these four Jumbles, one letter
to each square, to form four ordinary words.

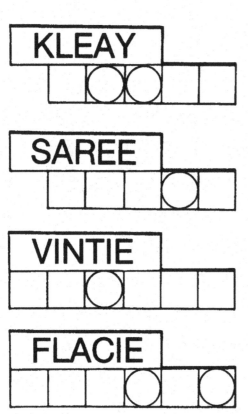

KLEAY

SAREE

VINTIE

FLACIE

He believes everything he hears

But it's in one ear and out the other

WHAT TOO MUCH OF AN OPEN MIND MIGHT BE LIKE.

Now arrange the circled letters
to form the surprise answer, as
suggested by the above cartoon.

Print answer here

JUMBLE®

Unscramble these four Jumbles, one letter to each square, to form four ordinary words.

PERPI

LEEXI

KAUMPE

PREMAT

ANOTHER NAME FOR A PAWNBROKER.

Now arrange the circled letters to form the surprise answer, as suggested by the above cartoon.

Print answer here A " ☐☐☐☐☐ ☐☐☐☐☐☐ "

JUMBLE®

Unscramble these four Jumbles, one letter to each square, to form four ordinary words.

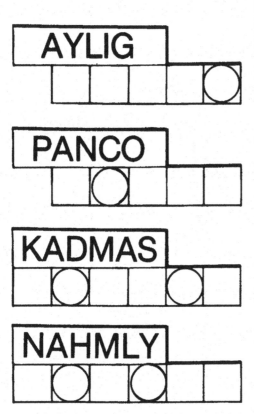

AYLIG

PANCO

KADMAS

NAHMLY

A GIRL WITH HORSE SENSE KNOWS WHEN TO DO THIS.

Now arrange the circled letters to form the surprise answer, as suggested by the above cartoon.

Print answer here

JUMBLE®

Unscramble these four Jumbles, one letter
to each square, to form four ordinary words.

TRUPE

ROFOL

LEUXED

GREESY

AT THE SEASHORE,
YOUR COMPOSURE
IS OFTEN DISTRACTED
BY THIS.

Now arrange the circled letters
to form the surprise answer, as
suggested by the above cartoon.

Print answer here

JUMBLE®

Unscramble these four Jumbles, one letter
to each square, to form four ordinary words.

THAPC

VILIC

UPCHIC

GAUHTT

WHAT A MARRIAGE
PROPOSAL IS.

Now arrange the circled letters
to form the surprise answer, as
suggested by the above cartoon.

Print answer
here

A

JUMBLE®

Unscramble these four Jumbles, one letter to each square, to form four ordinary words.

EMZIA

GINOG

ODUXTE

INCLEP

THE ONLY REASON THEY CALLED HIM A BIG SHOT WAS THAT HE WAS ALWAYS DOING THIS.

Now arrange the circled letters to form the surprise answer, as suggested by the above cartoon.

Print answer here

JUMBLE®

Unscramble these four Jumbles, one letter
to each square, to form four ordinary words.

DOBOL

KOPER

NUTHAG

GUMSED

WHAT THAT GOOD-
LOOKING DOG WAS.

Now arrange the circled letters
to form the surprise answer, as
suggested by the above cartoon.

Print answer here "◯◯◯◯◯◯◯◯◯"

JUMBLE®

Unscramble these four Jumbles, one letter to each square, to form four ordinary words.

TILOP

GACIM

RECUPS

CUNESS

He's always insulting people!

YOU'D GET NO PRAISES FROM THIS.

Now arrange the circled letters to form the surprise answer, as suggested by the above cartoon.

Print answer here AN " ⃝⃝⃝⃝⃝⃝⃝⃝⃝ "

JUMBLE®

Unscramble these four Jumbles, one letter to each square, to form four ordinary words.

NERTY

MILPE

HACTLE

SMABAL

WHERE ARMAMENTS MIGHT BE FOUND, NATURALLY.

Now arrange the circled letters to form the surprise answer, as suggested by the above cartoon.

Print answer here   AMONG " ☐☐☐ - ☐☐ - ☐☐☐☐ "

JUMBLE®

Unscramble these four Jumbles, one letter
to each square, to form four ordinary words.

BORNI

MILTI

TRIMAN

UNBOAD

He should
be mowing
the lawn

WHAT SHE CALLED
HER HUSBAND WHO
WAS AN AMATEUR
ORNITHOLOGIST.

Now arrange the circled letters
to form the surprise answer, as
suggested by the above cartoon.

Print answer here " ◯◯◯◯ ◯◯◯◯◯ "

JUMBLE®

Unscramble these four Jumbles, one letter
to each square, to form four ordinary words.

BOANT

LAGIE

JENNIO

RITHEH

She's never had to
worry about money

WHAT TO DO IN
ORDER TO HAVE
SOFT WHITE HANDS.

Now arrange the circled letters
to form the surprise answer, as
suggested by the above cartoon.

Print answer here

JUMBLE®

Unscramble these four Jumbles, one letter to each square, to form four ordinary words.

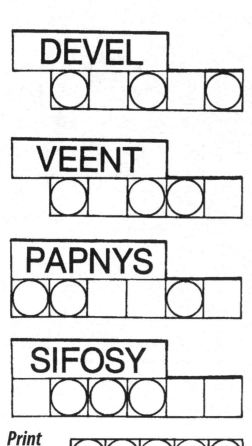

DEVEL

VEENT

PAPNYS

SIFOSY

ON THE AIR

WHAT THE NERVOUS DISC JOCKEY LIVES ON.

Now arrange the circled letters to form the surprise answer, as suggested by the above cartoon.

Print answer here

 &

JUMBLE®

Unscramble these four Jumbles, one letter to each square, to form four ordinary words.

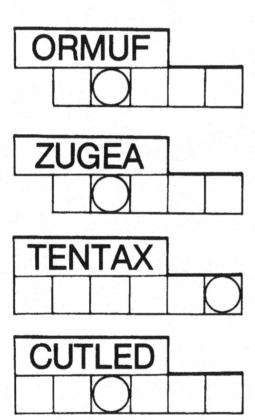

ORMUF

ZUGEA

TENTAX

CUTLED

And I thought I was doing great!

IRS

THE REASON SO MANY OF US ARE DISCONTENTED WITH OUR LOT THESE DAYS IS THAT IT'S NO LONGER THIS.

Now arrange the circled letters to form the surprise answer, as suggested by the above cartoon.

Print answer here

JUMBLE®

Unscramble these four Jumbles, one letter
to each square, to form four ordinary words.

YEEND

PREYK

SLIMIE

INTOAR

STEAKS and CHOPS

WHAT LIFE WAS FOR THE GUY WHO SPENT ALL HIS TIME AT THAT "SINGLES" SPOT.

Now arrange the circled letters
to form the surprise answer, as
suggested by the above cartoon.

Print
answer
here   JUST " ⃝⃝⃝⃝ " & ⃝⃝⃝⃝⃝

JUMBLE®

Unscramble these four Jumbles, one letter
to each square, to form four ordinary words.

DYMAL

ENDOM

NUDEAS

EMBLUF

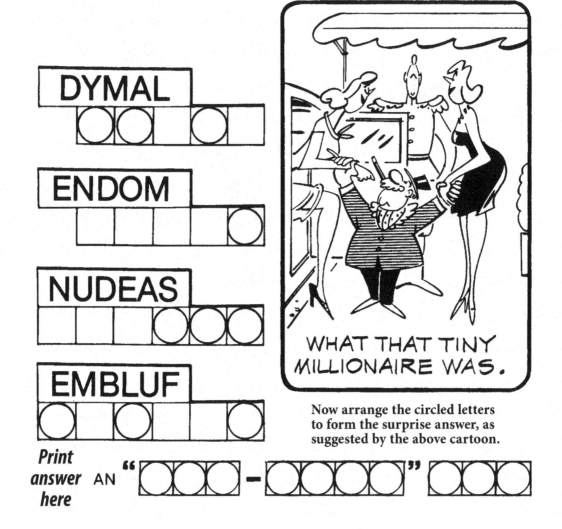

WHAT THAT TINY
MILLIONAIRE WAS.

Now arrange the circled letters
to form the surprise answer, as
suggested by the above cartoon.

Print
answer
here   AN   " ◯◯◯ - ◯◯◯◯◯ " ◯◯◯

JUMBLE®

Unscramble these four Jumbles, one letter
to each square, to form four ordinary words.

OEGOS

YETID

CHINLE

TINVER

MUCH OF
THE AUDIENCE
AT THAT OPERA
HOUSE WAS THIS.

Now arrange the circled letters
to form the surprise answer, as
suggested by the above cartoon.

Print answer here

JUMBLE®

Unscramble these four Jumbles, one letter
to each square, to form four ordinary words.

ROVLE

YOANN

TOOSHE

CUDREE

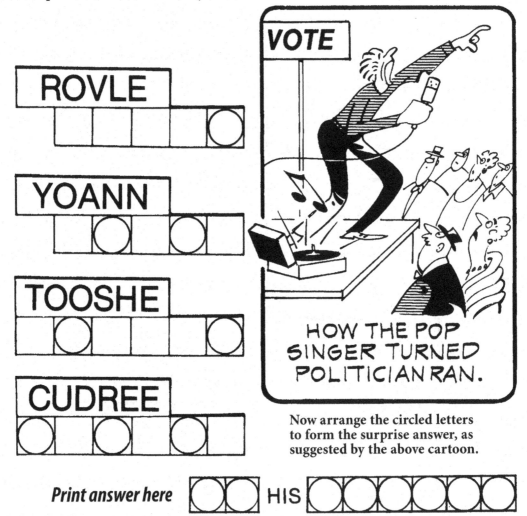

VOTE

HOW THE POP
SINGER TURNED
POLITICIAN RAN.

Now arrange the circled letters
to form the surprise answer, as
suggested by the above cartoon.

Print answer here ⬡⬡ HIS ⬡⬡⬡⬡⬡

JUMBLE®

Unscramble these four Jumbles, one letter
to each square, to form four ordinary words.

LEKAN

KECAD

RETINE

SURDIA

This is getting monotonous

WHAT A
VERY REPETITIVE
TYPE OF DANCE
MIGHT BE CALLED.

Now arrange the circled letters
to form the surprise answer, as
suggested by the above cartoon.

Print
answer
here   A "◯◯◯◯◯ – ◯◯◯◯◯"

JUMBLE®

Unscramble these four Jumbles, one letter
to each square, to form four ordinary words.

RISUV

CLEEX

NOOTIL

ARPITE

Oops!

WHAT AN ALIBI
USUALLY IS.

Now arrange the circled letters
to form the surprise answer, as
suggested by the above cartoon.

Print answer
here   A " ⬡⬡⬡⬡⬡ " ⬡⬡⬡⬡⬡⬡

JUMBLE®

Unscramble these four Jumbles, one letter to each square, to form four ordinary words.

FIGER

LASIA

AGMANE

RIMPER

THE **MARINES** WERE "ARRANGED" AS A STUDY GROUP.

Now arrange the circled letters to form the surprise answer, as suggested by the above cartoon.

Print answer here "  "

JUMBLE®

Unscramble these four Jumbles, one letter to each square, to form four ordinary words.

VOLEH

NISOB

CAMEZE

URBBUS

WHAT A GARBAGE TRUCK IS.

Now arrange the circled letters to form the surprise answer, as suggested by the above cartoon.

Print answer here A ⬡⬡⬡⬡ " ⬡⬡⬡⬡ "

JUMBLE®

Unscramble these four Jumbles, one letter
to each square, to form four ordinary words.

YEVAH

TAMID

YURTIP

INKELT

Not a drop of rain in sight

CRACK!

THE ONLY
REALLY RELIABLE
WEATHER "REPORT."

Now arrange the circled letters
to form the surprise answer, as
suggested by the above cartoon.

Print answer here

JUMBLE®

Unscramble these four Jumbles, one letter
to each square, to form four ordinary words.

TAUDI

GEALL

DRUTSY

INSORP

Wait—I've got connections!

WHAT TO DO WHEN CONFRONTED WITH A KNOTTY PROBLEM.

Now arrange the circled letters
to form the surprise answer, as
suggested by the above cartoon.

Print answer here

⚪⚪⚪⚪ ⚪⚪⚪⚪⚪⚪⚪

JUMBLE®

Unscramble these four Jumbles, one letter
to each square, to form four ordinary words.

MYNEE

DAMMA

TUILGY

DESEEC

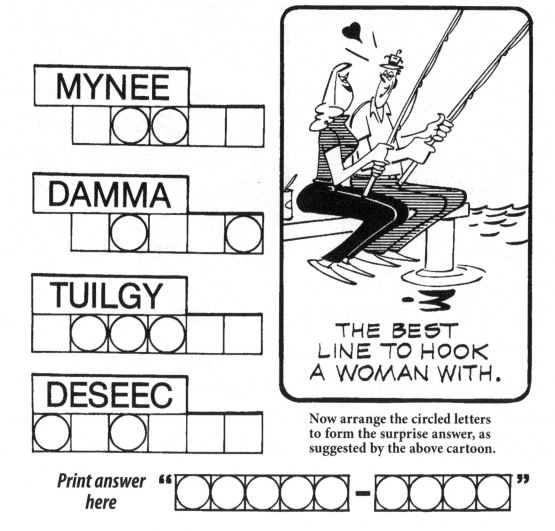

THE BEST
LINE TO HOOK
A WOMAN WITH.

Now arrange the circled letters
to form the surprise answer, as
suggested by the above cartoon.

Print answer
here " ⃝⃝⃝⃝⃝ – ⃝⃝⃝⃝ "

JUMBLE®

Unscramble these four Jumbles, one letter
to each square, to form four ordinary words.

LUPPI

PHOCE

CRESPO

LORFIC

P.D.

THEY MIGHT BE
UP CLOSE.

Now arrange the circled letters
to form the surprise answer, as
suggested by the above cartoon.

Print answer here " ☐☐☐☐☐☐☐ "

JUMBLE®

Unscramble these four Jumbles, one letter
to each square, to form four ordinary words.

NICCY

TAREF

DOAZIC

REMMEB

CONVENIENCE
DINNERS

WHAT THE PRICES
OF SOME OF
THOSE FROZEN FOODS
DEFINITELY WEREN'T.

Now arrange the circled letters
to form the surprise answer, as
suggested by the above cartoon.

Print answer here " ◯◯◯◯◯◯ "

137

JUMBLE®

Unscramble these four Jumbles, one letter
to each square, to form four ordinary words.

CEKOH

GURPE

RANCLE

MUBHEL

Have you decided yet where we're going?

SOMETHING A WOMAN FINDS EASIER TO DO WITH HER FACE THAN WITH HER MIND.

Now arrange the circled letters
to form the surprise answer, as
suggested by the above cartoon.

Print answer here

JUMBLE®

Unscramble these four Jumbles, one letter
to each square, to form four ordinary words.

AGGYB

NISHY

LIFTLE

YEKTUR

THE BIGGEST
PART OF THE FISH.

Now arrange the circled letters
to form the surprise answer, as
suggested by the above cartoon.

Print answer here ◯◯◯ " ◯◯◯◯ "

JUMBLE®

Unscramble these four Jumbles, one letter
to each square, to form four ordinary words.

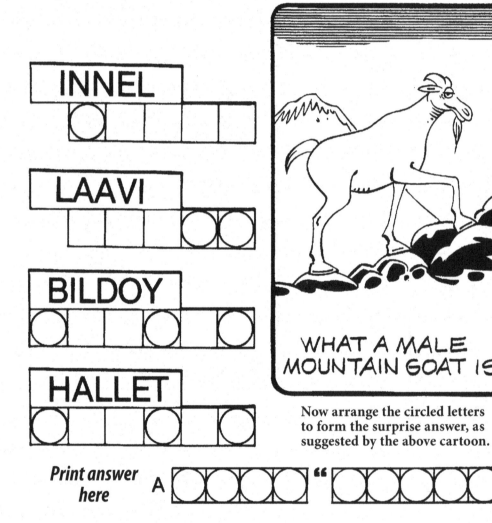

INNEL

LAAVI

BILDOY

HALLET

WHAT A MALE
MOUNTAIN GOAT IS.

Now arrange the circled letters
to form the surprise answer, as
suggested by the above cartoon.

**Print answer
here** A ⬡⬡⬡⬡⬡ " ⬡⬡⬡⬡⬡ "

JUMBLE®

Unscramble these four Jumbles, one letter
to each square, to form four ordinary words.

VUCER

NOFEL

LAFBLE

CALPEA

You'll have to
shape up

WHEN HE TOOK THAT
COURSE IN MARINE
BIOLOGY HIS
GRADES WERE THIS.

Now arrange the circled letters
to form the surprise answer, as
suggested by the above cartoon.

Print answer here   BELOW   " ◯ " ◯◯◯◯◯

JUMBLE®

Unscramble these four Jumbles, one letter
to each square, to form four ordinary words.

HACTY

TOSOP

AMRUTE

COPILY

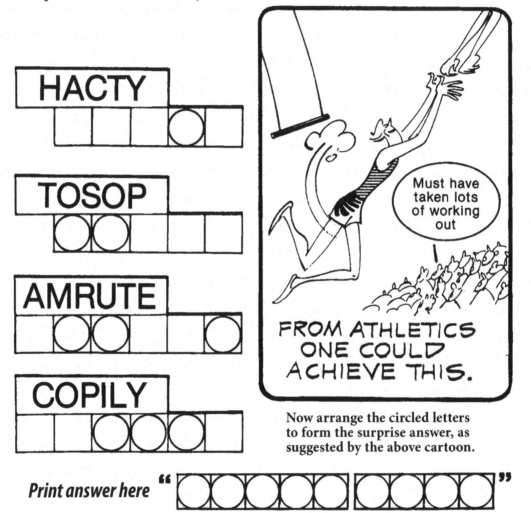

Must have
taken lots
of working
out

FROM ATHLETICS
ONE COULD
ACHIEVE THIS.

Now arrange the circled letters
to form the surprise answer, as
suggested by the above cartoon.

Print answer here "◯◯◯◯◯ ◯◯◯◯"

JUMBLE®

Unscramble these four Jumbles, one letter
to each square, to form four ordinary words.

PUMIO

ESKOT

NUTBOT

TALUCA

They say she's a snob

WHAT PINUP GIRLS
SOMETIMES ARE.

Now arrange the circled letters
to form the surprise answer, as
suggested by the above cartoon.

Print answer here ⬡⬡⬡⬡⬡ - ⬡⬡

JUMBLE®

Unscramble these four Jumbles, one letter
to each square, to form four ordinary words.

SHWIK

DARAW

SYPEDE

NEEGIN

WHAT THE CHURCH
SEXTON MINDS.

Now arrange the circled letters
to form the surprise answer, as
suggested by the above cartoon.

Print answer here   HIS ⬡⬡⬡⬡ & ⬡⬡⬡⬡

JUMBLE®

Unscramble these four Jumbles, one letter
to each square, to form four ordinary words.

RUFIT

ARBIN

NAUVEE

SLIMAD

WHILE SHE WAS
GETTING A FACEFUL
OF MUD SHE WAS
ALSO GETTING THIS.

Now arrange the circled letters
to form the surprise answer, as
suggested by the above cartoon.

Print
answer
here

AN ⬡⬡⬡⬡⬡⬡ OF " ⬡⬡⬡⬡ "

JUMBLE®

Unscramble these four Jumbles, one letter
to each square, to form four ordinary words.

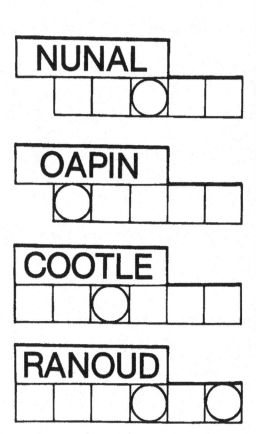

NUNAL

OAPIN

COOTLE

RANOUD

SKIING IS
A SPORT
IN WHICH SOME
END UP THIS WAY.

Now arrange the circled letters
to form the surprise answer, as
suggested by the above cartoon.

Print answer here

146

JUMBLE®

Unscramble these four Jumbles, one letter to each square, to form four ordinary words.

THOIS

ROGIN

COMIAT

EMSIDE

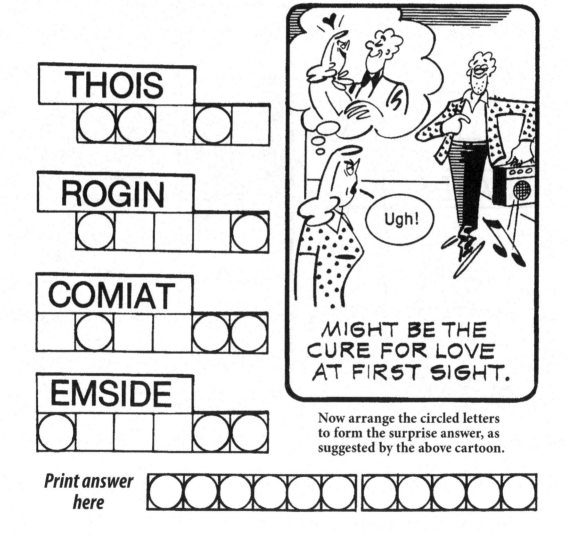

Ugh!

MIGHT BE THE
CURE FOR LOVE
AT FIRST SIGHT.

Now arrange the circled letters to form the surprise answer, as suggested by the above cartoon.

Print answer here

JUMBLE®

Unscramble these four Jumbles, one letter to each square, to form four ordinary words.

UGSIE

SAYES

MEENAC

SCEXIE

To our beloved boss!

WHAT SOME PEOPLE ENJOY DRINKING TO.

Now arrange the circled letters to form the surprise answer, as suggested by the above cartoon.

Print answer here

JUMBLE®

Unscramble these four Jumbles, one letter
to each square, to form four ordinary words.

RELIN

HATIF

NAPHOR

TALKEN

WHAT A SNOWBALL
MIGHT BE.

Now arrange the circled letters
to form the surprise answer, as
suggested by the above cartoon.

Print
answer
here

A "⬭⬭⬭⬭" ⬭⬭⬭⬭⬭⬭

JUMBLE®

Unscramble these four Jumbles, one letter
to each square, to form four ordinary words.

LUFAW

WUSAQ

DAYMAL

DELIJA

WHAT THERE
SEEMED TO
BE IN THAT
NOISY COURTROOM.

Now arrange the circled letters
to form the surprise answer, as
suggested by the above cartoon.

Print answer here MORE " ◯◯◯ " THAN ◯◯◯

JUMBLE®

Unscramble these four Jumbles, one letter
to each square, to form four ordinary words.

DRUGO

HERIK

BOINAL

WOBELL

WHAT THEY
SAID ABOUT THAT
EVENING GOWN.

Now arrange the circled letters
to form the surprise answer, as
suggested by the above cartoon.

Print
answer
here

" ⬡⬡⬡ ! — & ⬡⬡⬡⬡⬡⬡ "

JUMBLE®

Unscramble these four Jumbles, one letter
to each square, to form four ordinary words.

FLEAY

NUFTO

WRALEY

LOSTID

C'mon—get with it!

WHAT THE
GEOLOGIST WHO
SPECIALIZED IN
EARTHQUAKES WAS.

Now arrange the circled letters
to form the surprise answer, as
suggested by the above cartoon.

Print
answer
here

A " ⬡⬡⬡⬡⬡ " ⬡⬡⬡⬡⬡⬡

JUMBLE®

Unscramble these four Jumbles, one letter to each square, to form four ordinary words.

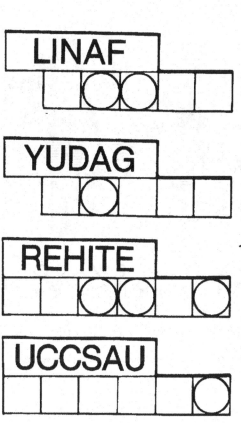

LINAF

YUDAG

REHITE

UCCSAU

Hmph!

THE ONLY THING A PESSIMIST EVER EXPECTS ON A SILVER PLATTER.

Now arrange the circled letters to form the surprise answer, as suggested by the above cartoon.

Print answer here

JUMBLE®

Unscramble these four Jumbles, one letter
to each square, to form four ordinary words.

NOCIT

NUMOR

TUPPIL

ENCOAB

Doesn't waste time

HE BECAME MAN OF
THE HOUR BECAUSE
HE KNEW HOW
TO MAKE THIS.

Now arrange the circled letters
to form the surprise answer, as
suggested by the above cartoon.

Print
answer
here   EVERY

JUMBLE®

Unscramble these four Jumbles, one letter
to each square, to form four ordinary words.

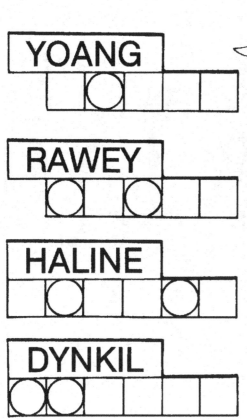

YOANG

RAWEY

HALINE

DYNKIL

Yak yak yak yak

?

THE BORE WOULDN'T
STOP TALKING
UNTIL HIS FRIEND
STARTED THIS.

Now arrange the circled letters
to form the surprise answer, as
suggested by the above cartoon.

Print answer here

JUMBLE®

Unscramble these four Jumbles, one letter
to each square, to form four ordinary words.

CINIG

ADEHA

TIMCAP

CORVEL

Must be some mistake

CHARGED
WITH SOMETHING
SHOCKING.

Now arrange the circled letters
to form the surprise answer, as
suggested by the above cartoon.

Print answer here

156

JUMBLE®

Unscramble these four Jumbles, one letter
to each square, to form four ordinary words.

YOWLL

LIRLT

HERNET

DINTUC

A SCRATCH PAD IS
FOR PEOPLE WHO
HAVE THIS AT ODD
TIMES AND PLACES.

Now arrange the circled letters
to form the surprise answer, as
suggested by the above cartoon.

*Print
answer
here*

THE ◯◯◯◯ TO ◯◯◯◯◯

JUMBLE®

Unscramble these four Jumbles, one letter
to each square, to form four ordinary words.

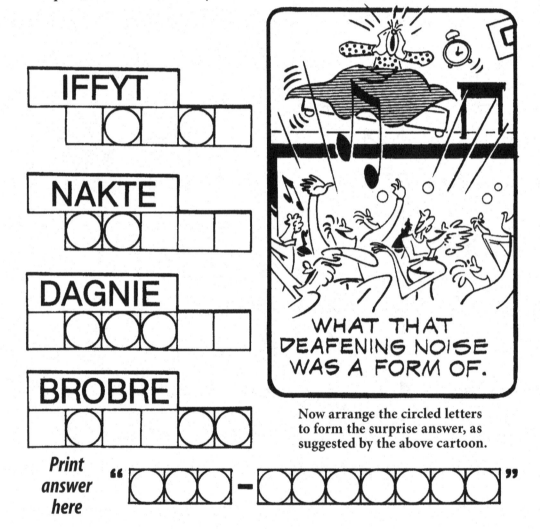

IFFYT

NAKTE

DAGNIE

BROBRE

WHAT THAT
DEAFENING NOISE
WAS A FORM OF.

Now arrange the circled letters
to form the surprise answer, as
suggested by the above cartoon.

*Print
answer
here*   " ◯◯◯ - ◯◯◯◯◯◯◯ "

JUMBLE®

Unscramble these four Jumbles, one letter to each square, to form four ordinary words.

TARFD

JOBUM

TENJUK

LETHEM

WHAT A DOG HOUSE IS.

Now arrange the circled letters to form the surprise answer, as suggested by the above cartoon.

Print answer here A

JUMBLE®

Unscramble these four Jumbles, one letter
to each square, to form four ordinary words.

VALGE

NALFK

SNODEC

DIMROB

DANCE

WHAT THE
BOUNCER AT
THAT COUNTRY AND
WESTERN CLUB WAS.

Now arrange the circled letters
to form the surprise answer, as
suggested by the above cartoon.

Print
answer A
here

"   "

JUMBLE.

Unscramble these four Jumbles, one letter
to each square, to form four ordinary words.

KUFLE

DOORE

LIFFUT

BLABED

WHAT COFFEE
OFTEN IS.

Now arrange the circled letters
to form the surprise answer, as
suggested by the above cartoon.

Print
answer
here

A " ◯◯◯◯◯ " ◯◯◯◯◯

JUMBLE®

Unscramble these four Jumbles, one letter
to each square, to form four ordinary words.

OGOIL

PHAMC

TABLLE

BIHRDY

Good they're
not driving
tonight

AULD LANG SYNE

WHAT NEW YEAR'S
EVE MIGHT BE
FOR SOME PEOPLE.

Now arrange the circled letters
to form the surprise answer, as
suggested by the above cartoon.

Print
answer AN "○○○○○○○○○○○○○○"
here

JUMBLE®

TIME MACHINE: 1984

CHALLENGER
PUZZLES

JUMBLE®

Unscramble these six Jumbles, one letter to each square, to form six ordinary words.

DUPLED

CLUBEK

TINISS

REUMED

EECCAD

INGOPE

WHAT DAVID DID TO GOLIATH.

Now arrange the circled letters to form the surprise answer, as suggested by the above cartoon.

Print answer here

" ⬡⬡⬡⬡⬡⬡ " HIM TO ⬡⬡⬡⬡⬡

JUMBLE®

Unscramble these six Jumbles, one letter to each square, to form six ordinary words.

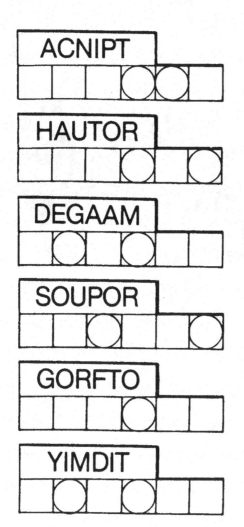

ACNIPT

HAUTOR

DEGAAM

SOUPOR

GORFTO

YIMDIT

THE KIND OF STORY THAT WOULDN'T INTEREST THIS GUY AT ALL.

Now arrange the circled letters to form the surprise answer, as suggested by the above cartoon.

Print answer here

A ⬡⬡⬡⬡ – ⬡⬡⬡⬡⬡⬡⬡ ONE

165

JUMBLE®

Unscramble these six Jumbles, one letter to each square, to form six ordinary words.

NIMEUM

LISHEC

CODJUN

SABDUR

DOUSEX

PEBICS

HOW THOSE SINGERS COMMUNICATED.

Now arrange the circled letters to form the surprise answer, as suggested by the above cartoon.

Print answer here

THEY " ⬡⬡⬡⬡⬡⬡⬡ – ⬡⬡⬡⬡⬡⬡⬡ "

JUMBLE®

Unscramble these six Jumbles, one letter
to each square, to form six ordinary words.

FELGUN

BERICK

YUNCAL

NAHRGE

DACUDE

CURSIC

WHAT THAT PHONY
BRAIN SURGEON
PRACTICED.

Now arrange the circled letters
to form the surprise answer, as
suggested by the above cartoon.

Print answer here

" ◯◯◯◯◯ ◯◯◯◯◯◯◯ "

JUMBLE®

Unscramble these six Jumbles, one letter to each square, to form six ordinary words.

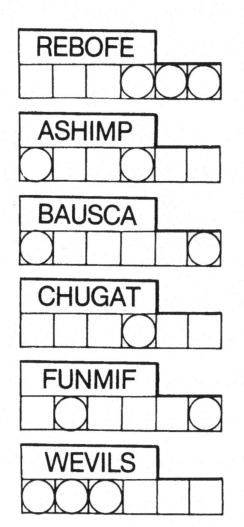

REBOFE

ASHIMP

BAUSCA

CHUGAT

FUNMIF

WEVILS

WHAT YOU SAW WHEN THOSE NEW NEXT-DOOR NEIGHBORS GAVE THEIR FIRST BIG PARTY.

Now arrange the circled letters to form the surprise answer, as suggested by the above cartoon.

Print answer here

THE ⬡⬡⬡⬡⬡⬡ ⬡⬡⬡⬡⬡⬡⬡⬡

JUMBLE®

Unscramble these six Jumbles, one letter to each square, to form six ordinary words.

TANGOU

BUNGIL

LAIFAC

GOIBLE

OURSEA

LAGYAX

We've been everywhere

WHAT THOSE PRETENTIOUS TRAVELERS RETURNED WITH PLENTY OF.

Now arrange the circled letters to form the surprise answer, as suggested by the above cartoon.

Print answer here

" ⬡⬡⬡⬡ & ⬡⬡⬡⬡⬡⬡⬡ "

JUMBLE®

Unscramble these six Jumbles, one letter to each square, to form six ordinary words.

THORPY

PARAPE

MOINCE

PERREF

REGLED

CASMIO

WHERE THE LUMBERJACK WENT BEFORE CHRISTMAS.

Now arrange the circled letters to form the surprise answer, as suggested by the above cartoon.

Print answer here

ON "   "
A

JUMBLE®

Unscramble these six Jumbles, one letter to each square, to form six ordinary words.

TAYFUL

MARKEB

LEHBED

ROQUIL

GOLFAN

SEDGIT

WHAT THE
SUCCESSFUL
REALTOR HAD.

Now arrange the circled letters to form the surprise answer, as suggested by the above cartoon.

Print answer here

" ◯◯◯◯ " TO BE ◯◯◯◯◯◯◯◯ FOR

JUMBLE®

Unscramble these six Jumbles, one letter
to each square, to form six ordinary words.

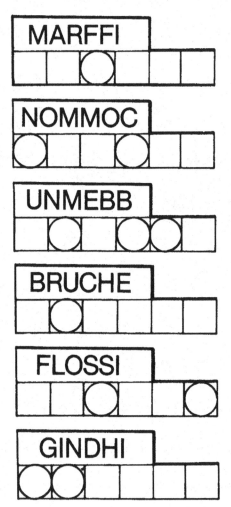

MARFFI

NOMMOC

UNMEBB

BRUCHE

FLOSSI

GINDHI

A very lonely man

WHAT THE
MISER KEPT.

Now arrange the circled letters
to form the surprise answer, as
suggested by the above cartoon.

Print answer here

TOO ⬭⬭⬭⬭ TO ⬭⬭⬭⬭⬭⬭⬭

JUMBLE®

Unscramble these six Jumbles, one letter to each square, to form six ordinary words.

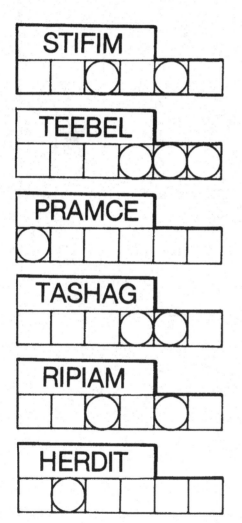

STIFIM

TEEBEL

PRAMCE

TASHAG

RIPIAM

HERDIT

If I say so myself, I'm terrific!

WHAT THAT EGOTISTICAL DOCTOR WAS.

Now arrange the circled letters to form the surprise answer, as suggested by the above cartoon.

Print answer here

AN " ☐ " ☐☐☐☐☐☐☐☐☐☐☐☐

JUMBLE®

Unscramble these six Jumbles, one letter
to each square, to form six ordinary words.

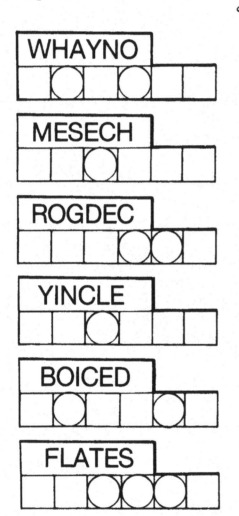

WHAYNO

MESECH

ROGDEC

YINCLE

BOICED

FLATES

IS THAT "SPOOK"
WHO'S RUNNING
FOR OFFICE LIKELY
TO GET ELECTED?

Now arrange the circled letters
to form the surprise answer, as
suggested by the above cartoon.

Print answer here

NOT A ⬡⬡⬡⬡⬡ OF A ⬡⬡⬡⬡⬡⬡

JUMBLE®

Unscramble these six Jumbles, one letter to each square, to form six ordinary words.

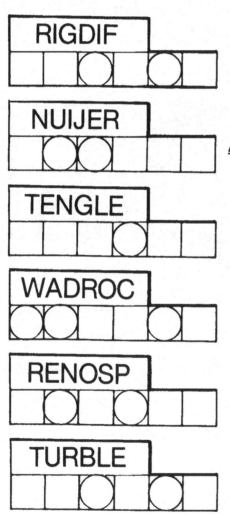

RIGDIF

NUIJER

TENGLE

WADROC

RENOSP

TURBLE

PRIVATE

WHAT THAT OVERLY PROTECTIVE OFFICE RECEPTIONIST WAS.

Now arrange the circled letters to form the surprise answer, as suggested by the above cartoon.

Print answer here

A

JUMBLE®

Unscramble these six Jumbles, one letter
to each square, to form six ordinary words.

HODRIC

KUPHOO

HAVEEB

LICIAT

REMIPE

TRUSEY

WHAT A
TAILGATER IS.

Now arrange the circled letters
to form the surprise answer, as
suggested by the above cartoon.

Print answer here

A

JUMBLE®

Unscramble these six Jumbles, one letter to each square, to form six ordinary words.

VINNET

HONUKO

GAYCEN

SMIHOD

MARLOF

LAPPOR

WHAT MANY A VETERAN PRIZE FIGHTER HAS BEEN.

Now arrange the circled letters to form the surprise answer, as suggested by the above cartoon.

Print answer here

◯◯◯◯◯◯◯ THE ◯◯◯◯◯

JUMBLE®

Unscramble these six Jumbles, one letter to each square, to form six ordinary words.

REDONP

STYLUB

PANOWE

ASTUNE

KORREB

BUTSOE

At least THIS is relaxing!

WHAT A MAN MIGHT TRY TO DO ON THE GOLF COURSE.

Now arrange the circled letters to form the surprise answer, as suggested by the above cartoon.

Print answer here

" ◯◯◯◯ " AWAY HIS ◯◯◯◯◯◯◯◯◯

JUMBLE®

Unscramble these six Jumbles, one letter to each square, to form six ordinary words.

INTYME

HETTER

NOVCOY

DREBIG

FONLEY

LIVRIE

Here—take it all! I don't want to get into any kind of trouble with the law!

IRS

A SMART INCOME TAX PAYER KNOWS THAT IT'S BETTER TO DO THIS.

Now arrange the circled letters to form the surprise answer, as suggested by the above cartoon.

Print answer here

⬡⬡⬡⬡ THAN ⬡⬡⬡⬡⬡⬡⬡

JUMBLE®

Unscramble these six Jumbles, one letter
to each square, to form six ordinary words.

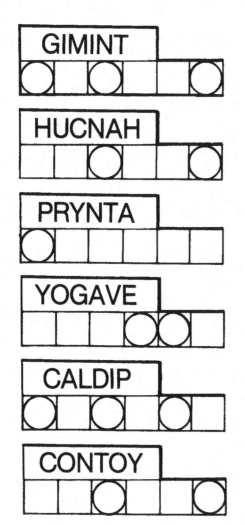

GIMINT

HUCNAH

PRYNTA

YOGAVE

CALDIP

CONTOY

Well! Glad to see you
at work for a change!

WHAT THE
CARTOGRAPHER WAS.

Now arrange the circled letters
to form the surprise answer, as
suggested by the above cartoon.

Print answer here

JUMBLE.

Unscramble these six Jumbles, one letter
to each square, to form six ordinary words.

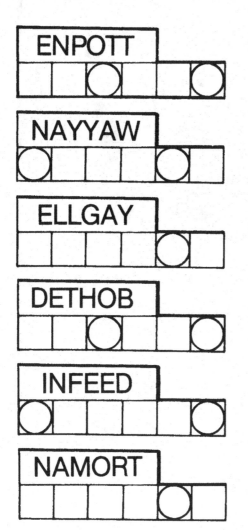

ENPOTT

NAYYAW

ELLGAY

DETHOB

INFEED

NAMORT

How about next Tuesday?

How about next month?

Next year?

Sorry, all booked up

WHAT KIND OF AN
EXISTENCE DID THAT
POPULAR GIRL LEAD?

Now arrange the circled letters
to form the surprise answer, as
suggested by the above cartoon.

Print answer here

A " ☐☐☐☐ - ☐☐ - ☐☐☐☐ " ONE

JUMBLE®

Unscramble these six Jumbles, one letter to each square, to form six ordinary words.

RECRON

KLARET

YONTUB

TUMPIE

UNCHAP

KUPPEE

AN USHERETTE SHOULD KNOW HOW TO DO THIS.

Now arrange the circled letters to form the surprise answer, as suggested by the above cartoon.

Print answer here

◯◯◯ A ◯◯◯ IN HIS ◯◯◯◯◯

JUMBLE®

Unscramble these six Jumbles, one letter to each square, to form six ordinary words.

RAUFIN

SWOBET

YERTAW

IPCINC

GANFIC

DITNIC

PROCESSING PLANT

Shh—don't disturb him

HOW THE ORANGE JUICE PRODUCER BECAME SO SUCCESSFUL.

Now arrange the circled letters to form the surprise answer, as suggested by the above cartoon.

Print answer here

BY " ◯◯◯◯◯◯◯◯◯◯◯◯◯ "

Answers

1. **Jumbles:** VITAL MUSIC NINETY FICKLE
Answer: Why he insisted on wearing seatbelts—
TO SAVE HIS KIN

2. **Jumbles:** CROUP LARVA HARROW BELONG
Answer: "How many pounds of limburger cheese do you want?"—A "PHEW"

3. **Jumbles:** NOBLE SHEAF GIGGLE INFECT
Answer: What that frustrated astronaut was always doing at home—BLASTING OFF

4. **Jumbles:** CASTE BRAND GUTTER ABDUCT
Answer: Although man does not live by bread alone, he may get by on this—"CRUST"

5. **Jumbles:** FORGO COVEY PYTHON ALKALI
Answer: What the "love affair" she was carrying on with all those soldiers must have been—"PLATOON-IC"

6. **Jumbles:** RURAL BANAL UNWISE IMPORT
Answer: A feeling you get when you open your mail on the first of the month—"BILL-IOUS"

7. **Jumbles:** VERVE BELLE TRAGIC AIRWAY
Answer: What they called the man who put glass into the igloo windows—THE "GLACIER"

8. **Jumbles:** EAGLE GASSY KITTEN MYSTIC
Answer: What that long tour made him—"SEE" SICK

9. **Jumbles:** SAVOR WRATH FELLOW EXEMPT
Answer: What his neighbor said when he showed off his new lawn equipment—"MOWER" POWER TO YOU

10. **Jumbles:** TOXIN MINUS HANGAR FIRING
Answer: What those boxers engaged in while having a few drinks—"INN" FIGHTING

11. **Jumbles:** DOUBT FOAMY EVOLVE NUDISM
Answer: When she asked for a diamond he turned this—"STONE" DEAF

12. **Jumbles:** BROIL RAJAH LIKELY POSTAL
Answer: Orthopedic surgeons must be lucky when they get this—ALL THE "BREAKS"

13. **Jumbles:** REBEL DIRTY FAMISH LACKEY
Answer: How she loved the cardiologist—WITH ALL HER HEART

14. **Jumbles:** CREEK MAXIM ASYLUM FLAXEN
Answer: What the robber said as he made his getaway—"SAFE" BY A MILE

15. **Jumbles:** NOISY GNOME SUBWAY KETTLE
Answer: Even more fun than having a vacation is having this—THE BOSS TAKE ONE

16. **Jumbles:** CATCH HEFTY FIZZLE GARBLE
Answer: What the guy who thought he was a wit was—ONLY HALF RIGHT

17. **Jumbles:** CHESS UNWED MISERY WALNUT
Answer: She admitted she was forty but she didn't do this—SAY WHEN

18. **Jumbles:** SOGGY ABASH PUZZLE RAVAGE
Answer: What he said that so-called barley soup was—BARELY SOUP

19. **Jumbles:** SHOWY WOMEN JACKET ALWAYS
Answer: What the talking cat said every time its master returned home—WHAT'S "MEW"?

20. **Jumbles:** JOKER MONEY PRAYER VALUED
Answer: What the down-and-out poet did—"ODE" EVERYONE

21. **Jumbles:** SWAMP BANJO RENDER MAGPIE
Answer: At what age were they married?—AT THE "PARSON-AGE"

22. **Jumbles:** GIVEN TWILL BAMBOO INFIRM
Answer: What the solitary pawnbroker undoubtedly was—A "LOANER"

23. **Jumbles:** BUILT MANGY JOVIAL TRYING
Answer: Could this be why he was a jailbird?—"ROBIN"

24. **Jumbles:** TITLE RIGOR GIMLET WINNOW
Answer: What happened to the bell that fell into the water?—IT WAS "RINGING" WET

25. **Jumbles:** AISLE NAIVE SUBDUE PUTRID
Answer: Why is venison so expensive?—IT'S "DEER"

26. **Jumbles:** BLANK TRACT MARAUD LEGUME
Answer: What happened to the plastic surgeon who was working in an overheated room?—HE MELTED

27. **Jumbles:** BROOD WHILE POORLY RADIUM
Answer: What's a parrot?—A WORDY BIRDIE

28. **Jumbles:** OZONE LLAMA PUNDIT QUEASY
Answer: Loves skin diving—A MOSQUITO

29. **Jumbles:** WHOSE CHEEK LIZARD SIZZLE
Answer: What his rich uncle who was a famous artist knew how to draw best—HIS WILL

30. **Jumbles:** LADLE DUSKY LOCALE CAMPUS
Answer: How the weighing machine tycoon started in business—ON A SMALL SCALE

31. **Jumbles:** MURKY OBESE UNCURL TYPIST
Answer: How to get your wife to bake those delicious rolls—BUTTER HER UP

32. **Jumbles:** DINER JUICY AMPERE FINITE
Answer: What the frightened rock was—"PETRIFIED"

33. **Jumbles:** DUCAT SOUSE CRAFTY KNOTTY
Answer: What to do when a plug doesn't fit—"SOCKET" (sock it)

34. **Jumbles:** LILAC GIANT TAWDRY NUANCE
Answer: What they were doing on that televised ballet—DANCING ON AIR

35. **Jumbles:** NIECE VIXEN LIMBER BENIGN
Answer: How the vampire loved—IN "VEIN"

36. **Jumbles:** SCARF JEWEL WIZARD BUCKET
Answer: If a shark is in the neighborhood, feed him this—JAWBREAKERS

37. **Jumbles:** OLDER FRANC YEARLY NAUSEA
Answer: What the umbrella merchant was saving his money for—A SUNNY DAY

38. **Jumbles:** BUMPY ACRID COBALT IODINE
Answer: How does Jack Frost get to work?—BY "ICICLE"

39. **Jumbles:** DRAWL COACH WHALER MUSKET
Answer: The ship docked near the barbershop because they all needed this—"CREW" CUTS

40. **Jumbles:** LIGHT HUSKY DECODE IRONIC
Answer: The turkey crossed the road to prove this—HE WASN'T CHICKEN

41. **Jumbles:** AWOKE RUMMY CACTUS PICKET
Answer: What the railroad man said to the hobo who was trying to steal a ride—MAKE TRACKS!

42. **Jumbles:** OUTDO CLEFT DREDGE HARBOR
Answer: What the secret agent was complaining of—A "CODE" IN THE HEAD

43. **Jumbles:** NOOSE DOWNY BAUBLE TYRANT
Answer: Why they had to put the vampire away—
92

HE WENT BATS

184

44. **Jumbles:** BLOOM FENCE MUSLIN LIQUID
Answer: What the doctor said when the patient complained of ringing in his ears—YOU'RE SOUND AS A BELL

45. **Jumbles:** IDIOT DOUSE JAGGED NUMBER
Answer: Why he quit working at the undertaker's—
IT WAS A DEAD-END JOB

46. **Jumbles:** DOILY BRAVO STICKY FOMENT
Answer: When a vandal made a hole in the fence at the nudist camp, the cops said they'd do this—LOOK INTO IT

47. **Jumbles:** RAPID CRAWL ICEBOX LARYNX
Answer: What he got when he read the story about those body snatchers—CARRIED AWAY

48. **Jumbles:** PHOTO SQUAB LEAVEN IMPUGN
Answer: What "HMS Pinafore" could undoubtedly be—
"NAME FOR SHIP"

49. **Jumbles:** KNEEL PROBE VORTEX LEGACY
Answer: What you might expect a pool-playing thief to do—
POCKET THE BALL

50. **Jumbles:** PAYEE WAFER BLITHE QUAVER
Answer: Why she dived into the sea—
TO GET A WAVE IN HER HAIR

51. **Jumbles:** JADED EVOKE NEARBY ELICIT
Answer: One cat told the other to be careful lest he do this—
END UP IN THAT RACKET

52. **Jumbles:** LANKY ORBIT CASKET ALPACA
Answer: What chiropractors can expect a lot of—BACK TALK

53. **Jumbles:** GLOVE DROOP JAUNTY HOMING
Answer: He decided to become an astronaut when his wife told him he was this—NO EARTHLY GOOD

54. **Jumbles:** NIPPY BASIN INTONE ADRIFT
Answer: If you want to start losing weight, you can get initiated from this—A "DIETITIAN"

55. **Jumbles:** PARCH FANCY ERMINE SURTAX
Answer: "Where do all the fleas go in winter?"—"SEARCH ME"

56. **Jumbles:** GRIME FAINT GLOOMY DRUDGE
Answer: The coffee tycoon decided to retire because he couldn't stand this—THE DAILY "GRIND"

57. **Jumbles:** SNACK FLORA JUGGLE PEPTIC
Answer: What he who laughs last often doesn't do—
GET THE JOKE

58. **Jumbles:** VYING WAGON MINGLE SNITCH
Answer: What the near-sighted boxer had trouble finding—
THE "WEIGH-IN"

59. **Jumbles:** HUMAN POWER DOUBLE WEASEL
Answer: What Eve said when Adam asked whether she still loved him—WHO ELSE?

60. **Jumbles:** EIGHT TRYST EYEFUL MORGUE
Answer: When is the cheapest time to phone your friends by long distance?—WHEN THEY'RE OUT

61. **Jumbles:** PORGY FRIAR HORROR ESTATE
Answer: "Did you hear my last joke?"—"I HOPE SO"

62. **Jumbles:** MEALY BARGE CHARGE TURNIP
Answer: What some bears seem to do in wintertime—
"HI-BEAR-NATE"

63. **Jumbles:** MOUTH TACKY DRAGON MYSELF
Answer: The man who stole a pudding was taken into this—
"CUSTARDY" (custody)

64. **Jumbles:** PAUSE FRAME EXTENT BOTHER
Answer: What was the trouble with the restaurant they opened up on the moon?—IT HAD NO "ATMOSPHERE"

65. **Jumbles:** FRAUD TAWNY HOURLY LAVISH
Answer: What he said when teacher gave him an "F" on the vocabulary test—WORDS FAIL ME

66. **Jumbles:** RUSTY EJECT MAINLY OPPOSE
Answer: Where you might find the schoolmaster—
IN "THE CLASSROOM"

67. **Jumbles:** SORRY BERTH STYLUS GRUBBY
Answer: What the man who was running in short bursts ended up with—BURST SHORTS

68. **Jumbles:** RAVEN NEWLY HECKLE MARMOT
Answer: What four-letter word do some people find most objectionable?—"WORK"

69. **Jumbles:** TRAIT OCCUR RABBIT WEAKEN
Answer: What the successful novelist must have been—
ON THE "WRITE" TRACK

70. **Jumbles:** DRAMA BEFOG UNSAID MAGNUM
Answer: From the surgeon came these words—"GO, NURSE!"

71. **Jumbles:** TROTH FOLIO IGUANA TUMULT
Answer: The impression made on one who's been in the Navy might be quite lasting—A TATTOO

72. **Jumbles:** PENCE OCTET HAZING CROUCH
Answer: Fishing may be a "disease," but it's not necessarily this—"CATCHING"

73. **Jumbles:** DUCHY JULEP PARISH BEMOAN
Answer: Did they call her this because she had a heart of stone?—A PEACH

74. **Jumbles:** BOGUS TOKEN MARLIN YEOMAN
Answer: What much so-called presidential timber often is—
MOSTLY "BARK"

75. **Jumbles:** LISLE UNCAP MUSCLE SQUALL
Answer: How that Don Juan treated all women—AS "SEQUELS"

76. **Jumbles:** FINIS HONEY HOOKED BUTANE
Answer: Where the conceited weight lifter let his body go—
TO HIS HEAD

77. **Jumbles:** CARGO KHAKI OUTLET MOTION
Answer: What that bakery tycoon was—ONE TOUGH COOKIE

78. **Jumbles:** MANGE SUAVE BEDECK PENURY
Answer: What her appeal sprang from—HER "EYE CUE"

79. **Jumbles:** DRYLY SYNOD ENTAIL BANGLE
Answer: What her ideal became after she married him—
AN ORDEAL

80. **Jumbles:** LAPEL OPERA COUSIN PACKET
Answer: What that old-time garage mechanic was bothered with—"CRANK" CALLS

81. **Jumbles:** CRIME MOGUL QUORUM BANISH
Answer: In which it's difficult to row—when you "manipulate" huge oars—A "ROUGH SEA"

82. **Jumbles:** CEASE PYLON CAJOLE INTACT
Answer: What the alert waiter always was—ON HIS "TIP" TOES

83. **Jumbles:** GRAVE FETID BOILED MANIAC
Answer: He thought his new computer was going to give him this kind of an illness—A "TERMINAL" ONE

84. **Jumbles:** GLOAT SUMAC INDUCE RADISH
Answer: What that crazy artist made his of his model—
A MUDDLE

85. **Jumbles:** FUSSY TASTY EXPOSE HAMMER
Answer: What a good history teacher should be—
A "PAST" MASTER

86. **Jumbles:** MERCY LUSTY TARGET NAPKIN
Answer: What a cent tip would certainly make these days—
A "PITTANCE"

87. **Jumbles:** DUNCE GUESS VOLUME QUAINT
Answer: A word of five letters the last four of which are unnecessary—"Q-UEUE"

88. **Jumbles:** PAGAN NOTCH BELIEF DEFACE
Answer: The sailor's many romances were just this—"FLEET-IN'

89. Jumbles: BILGE TEPID HUNTER FABLED
Answer: What to do when you get the feeling that you want to splurge—NIP IT IN THE "BUD-GET"

90. Jumbles: JUICE MAJOR EXPEND STYMIE
Answer: What the government expects to get from income taxes—"EXACT MONIES"

91. Jumbles: FLAKE VAGUE AMAZON EMERGE
Answer: Lightly gives you the go-ahead—GREEN

92. Jumbles: INLET TWINE FRENZY MALICE
Answer: What the author's pseudonym was—HIS "WRITE" NAME

93. Jumbles: FORCE HUMID TOWARD NEPHEW
Answer: What a sudden cloudburst is—A "DROWN" POUR

94. Jumbles: FLOUR WHEEL OPIATE BECALM
Answer: What she did every time she washed her hair—BLEW HER TOP

95. Jumbles: HAIRY SCOUR JUMPER ARMADA
Answer: What a sleepwalker's habit usually is—PAJAMAS

96. Jumbles: GULCH ROUSE PALATE GIBBET
Answer: What bathing girls might be—"IN SLIGHT GARB"

97. Jumbles: KINKY WALTZ BURIAL FACADE
Answer: What a quack doctor usually tries to do—DUCK THE LAW

98. Jumbles: TEASE OFTEN MASCOT SPLEEN
Answer: What the bankrupt businessman couldn't pass—THE "ASSET" TEST

99. Jumbles: ADULT TIGER BEFOUL GOVERN
Answer: What some secretaries have to take—A LOT FOR "GRUNTED"

100. Jumbles: TRIPE HOBBY STUCCO MEMORY
Answer: How you have to learn to take care of a baby—FROM THE BOTTOM UP

101. Jumbles: FAVOR PLUSH DEFAME BUSILY
Answer: Held up in bad weather—AN UMBRELLA

102. Jumbles: CRUSH WAKEN BISHOP NOTIFY
Answer: He's the most important man in the ring because he's the only one—WHO COUNTS

103. Jumbles: AGENT HYENA PURIFY RUBBER
Answer: What a fashion model might figure on—HER FIGURE

104. Jumbles: AGING FOYER BAFFLE GLOBAL
Answer: "Does it all come from an allergy?"—"LARGELY"

105. Jumbles: FLOOD SWOON WALLOP FINISH
Answer: What that Peeping Tom was—A WINDOW FAN

106. Jumbles: APPLY CHAIR DIVERT HUNGRY
Answer: What kind of youngster does basketball usually attract?—A VERY HIGH TYPE

107. Jumbles: FAIRY ELITE POWDER LAUNCH
Answer: What they called that crooked politician turned doctor—THE WARD "HEALER"

108. Jumbles: DITTO WHEAT TRICKY HALLOW
Answer: How children arrive at your door tonight—EVERY "WITCH" WAY

109. Jumbles: BASIC COCOA CALIPH FRIEZE
Answer: It's "said" to be a test—"ORAL"

110. Jumbles: LEAKY ERASE INVITE FACILE
Answer: What too much of an open mind might be like—A SIEVE

111. Jumbles: PIPER EXILE MAKEUP TAMPER
Answer: Another name for a pawnbroker—A "TIME KEEPER"

Jumbles: GAILY CAPON DAMASK HYMNAL
Answer: A girl with horse sense knows when to do this—"NAY"

113. Jumbles: ERUPT FLOOR DELUXE GEYSER
Answer: At the seashore, your composure is often distracted by this—EXPOSURE

114. Jumbles: PATCH CIVIL HICCUP TAUGHT
Answer: What a marriage proposal is—A HITCH PITCH

115. Jumbles: MAIZE GOING TUXEDO PENCIL
Answer: The only reason they called him a big shot was that he was always doing this—EXPLODING

116. Jumbles: BLOOD POKER NAUGHT SMUDGE
Answer: What that good looking dog was—"HOUNDSOME"

117. Jumbles: PILOT MAGIC SPRUCE CENSUS
Answer: You'd get no praises from this—AN "ASPERSION"

118. Jumbles: ENTRY IMPEL CHALET BALSAM
Answer: Where armaments might be found, naturally—AMONG "MEN-AT-ARMS"

119. Jumbles: ROBIN LIMIT MARTIN ABOUND
Answer: What she called her husband who was an amateur ornithologist—"BIRD BRAIN"

120. Jumbles: BATON AGILE ENJOIN HITHER
Answer: What to do in order to have soft white hands—NOTHING

121. Jumbles: DELVE EVENT SNAPPY OSSIFY
Answer: What the nervous disc jockey lives on—SPINS & NEEDLES

122. Jumbles: FORUM GAUZE EXTANT DULCET
Answer: The reason so many of us are discontented with our lot these days is that it's no longer this—A LOT

123. Jumbles: NEEDY PERKY SIMILE RATION
Answer: What life was for the guy who spent all his time at that "singles" spot—JUST "MEET" & DRINK

124. Jumbles: MADLY DEMON SUNDAE FUMBLE
Answer: What that tiny millionaire was—AN "ELF-MADE" MAN

125. Jumbles: GOOSE DEITY LICHEN INVERT
Answer: Much of the audience at that opera house was this—IN "TIERS" (tears)

126. Jumbles: LOVER ANNOY SOOTHE REDUCE
Answer: How the pop singer turned politician ran—ON HIS RECORD

127. Jumbles: ANKLE CAKED ENTIRE RADIUS
Answer: What a very repetitive type of dance might be called—A "REDUN-DANCE"

128. Jumbles: VIRUS EXCEL LOTION PIRATE
Answer: What an alibi usually is—A "SLIP" COVER

129. Jumbles: GRIEF ALIAS MANAGE PRIMER
Answer: The MARINES were "arranged" as a study group—"SEMINAR"

130. Jumbles: HOVEL BISON ECZEMA SUBURB
Answer: What a garbage truck is—A MESS "HAUL"

131. Jumbles: HEAVY ADMIT PURITY TINKLE
Answer: The only really reliable weather "report"—THUNDER

132. Jumbles: AUDIT LEGAL STURDY PRISON
Answer: What to do when confronted with a knotty problem—PULL STRINGS

133. Jumbles: ENEMY MADAM GUILTY SECEDE
Answer: The best line to hook a woman with—"MASCU-LINE"

134. Jumbles: PUPIL EPOCH CORPSE FROLIC
Answer: They might be UP CLOSE—"COUPLES"

135. Jumbles: CYNIC AFTER ZODIAC MEMBER
Answer: What the prices of some of those frozen foods definitely weren't—"FROZEN"

136. Jumbles: CHOKE PURGE LANCER HUMBLE
Answer: Something a woman finds easier to do with her face than with her mind—MAKE UP

137. Jumbles: BAGGY SHINY FILLET TURKEY
Answer: The biggest part of the fish—THE "TALK"

138. Jumbles: LINEN AVAIL BODILY LETHAL
Answer: What a male mountain goat is—A HILL "BILLY"

139. Jumbles: CURVE FELON BEFALL PALACE
Answer: When he took that course in marine biology his grades were this—BELOW "C" LEVEL

140. Jumbles: YACHT STOOP MATURE POLICY
Answer: From athletics one could achieve this—"LITHE ACTS"

141. Jumbles: OPIUM STOKE BUTTON ACTUAL
Answer: What pinup girls sometimes are—STUCK-UP

142. Jumbles: WHISK AWARD SPEEDY ENGINE
Answer: What the church sexton minds—HIS KEYS & PEWS

143. Jumbles: FRUIT BRAIN AVENUE DISMAL
Answer: While she was getting a faceful of mud she was also getting this—AN EARFUL OF "DIRT"

144. Jumbles: ANNUL PIANO OCELOT AROUND
Answer: Skiing is a sport in which some end up this way—END UP

145. Jumbles: HOIST GROIN ATOMIC DEMISE
Answer: Might be the cure for love at first sight—SECOND SIGHT

146. Jumbles: GUISE ESSAY MENACE EXCISE
Answer: What some people enjoy drinking to—EXCESS

147. Jumbles: LINER FAITH ORPHAN ANKLET
Answer: What a snowball might be—A "PANE" KILLER

148. Jumbles: AWFUL SQUAW MALADY JAILED
Answer: What there seemed to be in that noisy courtroom—MORE "JAW" THAN LAW

149. Jumbles: GOURD HIKER ALBINO BELLOW
Answer: What they said about that evening gown—"LOW!—& BEHOLD"

150. Jumbles: LEAFY FOUNT LAWYER STOLID
Answer: What the geologist who specialized in earthquakes was—A "FAULT" FINDER

151. Jumbles: FINAL GAUDY EITHER CAUCUS
Answer: The only thing a pessimist ever expects on a silver platter—TARNISH

152. Jumbles: TONIC MOURN PULPIT BEACON
Answer: He became man of the hour because he knew how to make this—EVERY MINUTE COUNT

153. Jumbles: AGONY WEARY INHALE KINDLY
Answer: The bore wouldn't stop talking until his friend started this—WALKING

154. Jumbles: ICING AHEAD IMPACT CLOVER
Answer: Charged with something shocking—ELECTRIC

155. Jumbles: LOWLY TRILL NETHER INDUCT
Answer: A scratch pad is for people who have this at odd times and places—THE ITCH TO WRITE

156. Jumbles: FIFTY TAKEN GAINED ROBBER
Answer: What that deafening noise was a form of—"EAR-ITATION"

157. Jumbles: DRAFT JUMBO JUNKET HELMET
Answer: What a dog house is—A MUTT HUT

158. Jumbles: GAVEL FLANK SECOND MORBID
Answer: What the bouncer at that country and western club was—A FOLK "SLINGER"

159. Jumbles: FLUKE RODEO FITFUL DABBLE
Answer: What coffee often is—A "BREAK" FLUID

160. Jumbles: IGLOO CHAMP BALLET HYBRID
Answer: What New Year's Eve might be for some people—AN "ALCOHOLIDAY"

161. Jumbles: PUDDLE BUCKLE INSIST DEMURE ACCEDE PIGEON
Answer: Wha t David did to Goliath—"ROCKED" HIM TO SLEEP

162. Jumbles: CATNIP AUTHOR DAMAGE POROUS FORGOT DIMITY
Answer: The kind of story that wouldn't interest this guy at all—A HAIR-RAISING ONE

163. Jumbles: IMMUNE CHISEL JOCUND ABSURD EXODUS BICEPS
Answer: How those singers communicated—THEY "CHORUS-PONDED"

164. Jumbles: ENGULF BICKER LUNACY HANGER ADDUCE CIRCUS
Answer: What that phony brain surgeon practiced—"SKULL DUGGERY"

165. Jumbles: BEFORE MISHAP ABACUS CAUGHT MUFFIN SWIVEL
Answer: What you saw when those new next-door neighbors gave their first big party—THE HOUSE SWARMING

166. Jumbles: NOUGAT BLUING FACIAL OBLIGE AROUSE GALAXY
Answer: What those pretentious travelers returned with plenty of—"BRAG & BAGGAGE"

167. Jumbles: TROPHY APPEAR INCOME PREFER LEDGER MOSAIC
Answer: Where the lumberjack went before Christmas—ON A "CHOPPING" SPREE

168. Jumbles: FAULTY EMBARK BEHELD LIQUOR FLAGON DIGEST
Answer: What the successful realtor had—"LOTS" TO BE THANKFUL FOR

169. Jumbles: AFFIRM COMMON BENUMB CHERUB FOSSIL HIDING
Answer: What the miser kept—TOO MUCH TO HIMSELF

170. Jumbles: MISFIT BEETLE CAMPER AGHAST IMPAIR DITHER
Answer: What that egotistical doctor was—AN "I" SPECIALIST

171. Jumbles: ANYHOW SCHEME CODGER NICELY BODICE FESTAL
Answer: Is that "spook" who's running for office likely to get elected?—NOT A GHOST OF A CHANCE

172. Jumbles: FRIGID INJURE GENTLE COWARD PERSON BUTLER
Answer: What that overly protective office receptionist was—A REJECTIONIST

173. Jumbles: ORCHID HOOKUP BEHAVE ITALIC EMPIRE SURETY
Answer: What a tailgater is—A BUMPER STICKER

174. Jumbles: INVENT UNHOOK AGENCY MODISH FORMAL POPLAR
Answer: What many a veteran prize fighter has been—THROUGH THE ROPES

175. Jumbles: PONDER SUBTLY WEAPON UNSEAT BROKER OBTUSE
Answer: What a man might try to do on the golf course—"PUTT" AWAY HIS TROUBLES

176. Jumbles: ENMITY TETHER CONVOY BRIDGE FELONY VIRILE
Answer: A smart income tax payer knows that it's better to do this—GIVE THAN DECEIVE

177. Jumbles: TIMING HAUNCH PANTRY VOYAGE PLACID TYCOON
Answer: What the cartographer was—CAUGHT MAPPING

178. Jumbles: POTENT ANYWAY GALLEY HOTBED DEFINE MATRON
Answer: What kind of an existence did that popular girl lead?—A "DATE-TO-DATE" ONE

179. Jumbles: CORNER TALKER BOUNTY IMPUTE PAUNCH UPKEEP
Answer: An usherette should know how to do this—PUT A MAN IN HIS PLACE

180. Jumbles: UNFAIR BESTOW WATERY PICNIC FACING INDICT
Answer: How the orange juice producer became so successful—BY "CONCENTRATING"

187

Need More Jumbles®?

Jumble® Books

More than 175 puzzles each!

Cowboy Jumble®
$10.95 • ISBN: 978-1-62937-355-3

Jammin' Jumble®
$9.95 • ISBN: 978-1-57243-844-6

Java Jumble®
$10.95 • ISBN: 978-1-60078-415-6

Jet Set Jumble®
$9.95 • ISBN: 978-1-60078-353-1

Jolly Jumble®
$10.95 • ISBN: 978-1-60078-214-5

Jumble® Anniversary
$10.95 • ISBN: 987-1-62937-734-6

Jumble® Ballet
$10.95 • ISBN: 978-1-62937-616-5

Jumble® Birthday
$10.95 • ISBN: 978-1-62937-652-3

Jumble® Celebration
$10.95 • ISBN: 978-1-60078-134-6

Jumble® Champion
$10.95 • ISBN: 978-1-62937-870-1

Jumble® Coronation
$10.95 • ISBN: 978-1-62937-976-0

Jumble® Cuisine
$10.95 • ISBN: 978-1-62937-735-3

Jumble® Drag Race
$9.95 • ISBN: 978-1-62937-483-3

Jumble® Ever After
$10.95 • ISBN: 978-1-62937-785-8

Jumble® Explorer
$9.95 • ISBN: 978-1-60078-854-3

Jumble® Explosion
$10.95 • ISBN: 978-1-60078-078-3

Jumble® Farm
$10.95 • ISBN: 978-1-63727-460-6

Jumble® Fever
$9.95 • ISBN: 978-1-57243-593-3

Jumble® Galaxy
$10.95 • ISBN: 978-1-60078-583-2

Jumble® Garden
$10.95 • ISBN: 978-1-62937-653-0

Jumble® Genius
$10.95 • ISBN: 978-1-57243-896-5

Jumble® Geography
$10.95 • ISBN: 978-1-62937-615-8

Jumble® Getaway
$10.95 • ISBN: 978-1-60078-547-4

Jumble® Gold
$10.95 • ISBN: 978-1-62937-354-6

Jumble® Health
$10.95 • ISBN: 978-1-63727-085-1

Jumble® Heist
$11.95 • ISBN: 978-1-63727-461-3

Jumble® Jackpot
$10.95 • ISBN: 978-1-57243-897-2

Jumble® Jailbreak
$9.95 • ISBN: 978-1-62937-002-6

Jumble® Jambalaya
$9.95 • ISBN: 978-1-60078-294-7

Jumble® Jitterbug
$10.95 • ISBN: 978-1-60078-584-9

Jumble® Journey
$10.95 • ISBN: 978-1-62937-549-6

Jumble® Jubilation
$10.95 • ISBN: 978-1-62937-784-1

Jumble® Jubilee
$10.95 • ISBN: 978-1-57243-231-4

Jumble® Juggernaut
$9.95 • ISBN: 978-1-60078-026-4

Jumble® Kingdom
$10.95 • ISBN: 978-1-62937-079-8

Jumble® Knockout
$9.95 • ISBN: 978-1-62937-078-1

Jumble® Madness
$10.95 • ISBN: 978-1-892049-24-7

Jumble® Magic
$9.95 • ISBN: 978-1-60078-795-9

Jumble® Mania
$10.95 • ISBN: 978-1-57243-697-8

Jumble® Marathon
$9.95 • ISBN: 978-1-60078-944-1

Jumble® Masterpiece
$10.95 • ISBN: 978-1-62937-916-6

Jumble® Neighbor
$10.95 • ISBN: 978-1-62937-845-9

Jumble® Parachute
$10.95 • ISBN: 978-1-62937-548-9

Jumble® Party
$10.95 • ISBN: 978-1-63727-008-0

Jumble® Safari
$9.95 • ISBN: 978-1-60078-675-4

Jumble® School
$11.95 • ISBN: 978-1-63727-328-9

Jumble® Sensation
$10.95 • ISBN: 978-1-60078-548-1

Jumble® Skyscraper
$10.95 • ISBN: 978-1-62937-869-5

Jumble® Symphony
$10.95 • ISBN: 978-1-62937-131-3

Jumble® Theater
$9.95 • ISBN: 978-1-62937-484-0

Jumble® Time Machine: 1972
$10.95 • ISBN: 978-1-63727-082-0

Jumble® Time Machine: 1984
$12.95 • ISBN: 978-1-63727-389-0

Jumble® Time Machine: 1993
$10.95 • ISBN: 978-1-63727-293-0

Jumble® Trouble
$10.95 • ISBN: 978-1-62937-917-3

Jumble® University
$10.95 • ISBN: 978-1-62937-001-9

Jumble® Unleashed
$10.95 • ISBN: 978-1-62937-844-2

Jumble® Vacation
$10.95 • ISBN: 978-1-60078-796-6

Jumble® Wedding
$9.95 • ISBN: 978-1-62937-307-2

Jumble® Workout
$10.95 • ISBN: 978-1-60078-943-4

Jump, Jive and Jumble®
$9.95 • ISBN: 978-1-60078-215-2

Lunar Jumble®
$9.95 • ISBN: 978-1-60078-853-6

Monster Jumble®
$10.95 • ISBN: 978-1-62937-213-6

Mystic Jumble®
$9.95 • ISBN: 978-1-62937-130-6

Rainy Day Jumble®
$10.95 • ISBN: 978-1-60078-352-4

Royal Jumble®
$10.95 • ISBN: 978-1-60078-738-6

Sports Jumble®
$10.95 • ISBN: 978-1-57243-113-3

Summer Fun Jumble®
$10.95 • ISBN: 978-1-57243-114-0

Touchdown Jumble®
$9.95 • ISBN: 978-1-62937-212-9

Oversize Jumble® Books

More than 500 puzzles!

...ssal Jumble®
...N: 978-1-57243-490-5

Jumbo Jumble®
$19.95 • ISBN: 978-1-57243-314-4

Jumble® Crosswords™

More than 175 puzzles!

Jumble® Crosswords™
$10.95 • ISBN: 978-1-57243-347-2